THINK LIKE A
BILLIONAIRE

BECOME A
BILLIONAIRE

AS A MAN THINKS, SO IS HE

THINK LIKE A
BILLIONAIRE

BECOME A
BILLIONAIRE

AS A MAN THINKS, SO IS HE

SCOT ANDERSON

Harrison House
Tulsa, OK

15 14 13 12   10 9 8 7 6 5 4 3 2 1

Think Like a Billionaire, Become a Billionaire
As a Man Thinks, So Is He
ISBN: 978-1-68031-376-5
Copyright © 2012 by Scot Anderson

Published by Harrison House Publishers, Inc.

DEDICATION

I dedicate this book to my wife, without whom I would never be who I am today. My success is due to you and your unconditional love. You are the most valuable thing in my life. You are my best friend and truly the greatest gift God has ever given to me.

I love you now, and forever.

TABLE OF CONTENTS

A NOTE FROM THE AUTHOR

I am so glad you purchased the expanded version of *Think Like a Billionaire*. I learned so much since the original book came out that I had always wished I could go back and put in. Well, here I get the opportunity. I know you will enjoy the life-changing information that I was able to add along with the additional chapters.

I think the greatest addition to this book is the video teachings that accompany the book. This allows me to really expand on the material, and really mentor you on how to think like a billionaire. It also makes the book more personable and allows me to be constantly updating and changing this book. As I learn, you learn. Each chapter has a teaching to go along with it. I will also be adding additional teachings and additional chapters for you to download from time to time. You will also have access to these teachings on podcast. Simply go to www.lifewithscot.com and follow the links.

Let's embark on this journey together. As a millionaire once said to me, "Now is the time to start your journey towards wealth. Most people wait until tomorrow to do what they can do today. Those people never get past just getting by." Let's start our journey now!

1
ONE CHANGE WILL PRODUCE WEALTH

*E*veryone thinks of changing the world, but no
one thinks of changing himself.

-Leo Tolstoy

After interviewing numerous multi-millionaires, reading more than twenty books on becoming a millionaire, and listening to nearly 400 hours of CDs on becoming wealthy, I have come to a conclusion—a conclusion that literally changed my life in just one year. A conclusion that took me from having a net worth of maybe $250,000, that is, if I sold everything—the 401(k), the equity in the house, even the kids—to over $3,000,000 in just one year. That's a net worth more than twelve times where I started, with another $15,000,000 worth of projects in the works. If I continue on that pace, I should be a billionaire in the next five to ten years.

What is interesting is that it took only one change, only one thing that I had to do differently. That one thing is what this book is all about. If you apply what you learn in this book, you will follow the exact same one-year journey. If you do this one thing, you, too, will be on your way to becoming a billionaire.

The one thing is so simple, yet I spent thirty-seven years of my life avoiding it. It was so easy, yet it is the one thing we all avoid. I had to change the way I thought. Yes, that is it. When I changed the way I thought, I began to change what I did, which then changed the results in my life. It was so simple, yet it took thirty-seven years for me to grab hold of it and actually do it.

Proverbs 23:7 says that as a man thinks, so is he. If I begin to think like a billionaire, according to the Bible, my life has no choice but to produce it. Where you are today is a result of the thoughts you had yesterday; where you go tomorrow is based on your thoughts today. If you can think like the 5% who are the wealthy, in a matter of time, you will be part of the 5%. If you continue to think like the 95%, which represents the average person, you will remain average. You will live a life of just enough—save just enough to retire, maybe get a Winnebego, and live off your 401(k) and your Social Security. But if you start thinking like a billionaire, you begin to step into the area God wants you to be in, the land of abundance.

Jesus said that out of the abundance of your heart, you produce. Whatever is in your heart will create the world you live in. If average is in your heart, if just get by is in your heart, then that is what will produce itself. If abundance is in your heart, then abundance will create itself in your world.

After all the interviews, all the books, all the CDs, when I cut through all the silly get rich gimmicks, the tricks that do not work, when I really boiled it all down, I found out that the wealthy think differently than the rest of us. That is why you could take all of Donald Trump's money away and in just a short amount of time, because of the way he thinks, he would be right back where he is today. How Trump thinks, so is he.

Billionaires think differently. They think differently about seven things in particular: Money, Investing, Jobs, Risks, Wisdom, Time and Problems.

Money

Billionaires think differently about what money is for. We see money as a way to get things. They see money as a tool to invest. We need more to get a bigger house, a nicer car, a bigger TV. Billionaires see money as a tool to be used to make more money. Once they get an abundance, a por-

> **We buy out of our lack. They buy out of their abundance.**

tion of that is used for the finer things in life. Billionaires use a little for the extras of life, and a major portion to create an abundance for life. We use a major portion for the things of life, and a little bit to invest (into 401(k)s, a little to dabble in the stock market) so we can get by in life.

As soon as we get some extra money, we look to where we can spend it. The rich immediately look to where they can invest it. We finally get that raise and right away we go out and get a nicer car because we can now afford an extra $250 car payment. We can now go down and get that big screen TV and make payments on it for the next five years. The wealthy, when they first start, say, "We'll drive what we are driving, watch what we are watching, and through investing, turn that $250 a month into millions. Then we can buy those things out of our abundance." We buy out of our lack. They buy out of their abundance.

The rich see money as a tool.
We see money as a way to buy stuff.

We buy today, and pay a lot more tomorrow. They invest today, and buy a lot more tomorrow.

*A*ll riches have their origin in the mind. Wealth is in ideas - not money.

-*Robert Collier*

Investing

We see investing as something we do just to have enough to retire. The wealthy see it as something you do to give you an abundance. We invest in 401(k)s and maybe a little bit in stocks (off of a tip someone who knows nothing about stocks gave us). We know nothing about investing, so we tend not to do it very well.

The wealthy see investing as a priority, so they are constantly reading, studying, and learning all they can about investing. The rest of us glance at the business section and read a report or two on Yahoo stock. The wealthy spend a significant portion of their lives learning how to be great investors. We spend a moment of time reading about how the wealthy made their money investing, all the while saying, "How come that never happens to me? That guy got so lucky!" No, he wasn't lucky; he was prepared. LUCK always favors the prepared. He thought differently, and that different thinking made him lucky.

To us, investing isn't a priority. Because it is not a priority, we don't have much to invest with. Investing isn't even something we budget into our lives. We budget for clothes, going out, vacations, TVs, golf clubs and all the stuff in life. The rich, when they got started, budgeted around their investments. We budget around our stuff.

> **The rich, when they got started, budgeted around their investments. We budget around our stuff.**

We see investing as a means for retirement. The wealthy see it as a way to catapult them into abundance. For them, investing is the key to abundance. To us, investing is the key to having just enough when we retire.

Jobs

We think that if we could just get a better job, we would be rich. What is funny is that if Trump lost his money, I guarantee that finding a great job would not be his priority. Trump would be looking for an investment.

The rich believe that your money should work for you. We believe that we should work for our money.

"Oh, if I just had a better job. If I could just get that promotion, I would be rich."

No, you would make more money, but you would not be rich. I know people who make six figure salaries who, if they sold everything they have, would have a net worth under a few hundred thousand dollars. Yes, they have the big house, the big car, all the perks of life. Yet they are not wealthy. I have seen it happen so many times where a person making $200,000 a year loses the job and loses everything. Sports stars, making millions a year, end their careers and file bankruptcy. I have heard that nearly 75% of all NFL football players claim bankruptcy after they stop playing.

The wealthy saw their jobs as a tool to get money to invest. We see our jobs as a tool to get money for stuff. Think about it. You probably make $20,000 to $30,000 more a year than you did ten years ago. Where is the money? What did you do with last year's $5,000 raise? Bigger TV? A boat? A car? Maybe you don't even know. Ten years ago, at the end of the month, after paying all the bills, you had $37 left over. Today, when you are making nearly twice as much, you have $37 left over. Unless you change your thinking, ten years from now, you will have $37 left over.

Unless we change our thinking, it will not matter how much money we make. We will never become wealthy.

If Trump lost all of his money, he would not go looking for a great job to make his millions. He might get a job, but the purpose of the job would be to give him money to invest. That is the purpose of your job. To the wealthy person, the job is there strictly to maintain your current living situation while giving you as much money to invest as possible—because it will be the investing that produces wealth, not the job.

We have to begin to see our money as seed to be sown. The Bible says that God gives seed to the sower (2 Corinthians 9:10). That doesn't just mean He gives to the person who sows into the church. It also means He gives to the person who sows into investments. Consider the parable of the talents. What happened to the guy who just held onto his money? It was taken away and given to the one who invested.

Look around you. Who is the money being given to? The one who is sowing it, not the one who is hoarding it or spending it. Most of us, because we

> **If Trump lost all of his money, he would not go looking for a great job.**

have the same attitude as the one who lost his money, say, "But I was afraid to invest. I was afraid I would lose it." Because of that thinking, we never get the abundance we should have.

When we think that our jobs will give us economical freedom, we have taken God and put Him into a box. We take a limitless God and put limits on Him. There is one thing God cannot do and that is go against the will of a person. I don't care how much you pray and fast, put on sackcloth and run around, God cannot make your boss give you a raise. God cannot make your boss promote you. Your boss will not wake up one morning and go, "You know what? Scot isn't that good of an employee, but I think I will cut my own salary and give him a big raise." Do you see how God is limited?

But if you begin to invest, God says, "Now I have something to work with." You have now taken God out of the box and said, "God, You are limitless. Do Your thing."

God says, "I give seed to the sower." He says, "Scot was faithful with the little I gave him. I will make him ruler over much." The Bible says that God will bless whatever you put your hands to. The problem is that most of us are only putting our hands on our remote control. And yes, we do have the best TV around. But when you start to put your hands into investments, God begins to pour out into all your endeavors.

Risks

We don't take risks because we are afraid we will fail. What if it doesn't work? The rich think that if they don't take risks, they have already failed.

We ask, "What if the business goes belly up? I will be a failure." The rich think, "If I don't take a chance on the business, I am a failure."

We live in a world that has God unemployed. We make all our bill payments, our VISA and MasterCard payments and car payments. We can do all that on our own. We really don't need God.

God so desperately wants us in a place where we need Him, where we step out and say, "Okay, God, for me, this is impossible. But with You, nothing is impossible." In doing this, I have employed God. I have given Him something to do in my life. We are now working together. The Bible says that God directs our steps. It doesn't say He directs our sitting. We don't just sit back and wait for God to drop a million-dollar idea in our laps. We start to step out. Once we take some steps, God can say, "Okay, go this way. Now turn this way."

My dad always said that you cannot steer a bicycle that is not moving. It is time we get that bicycle going. It is time we step out and take some risks. The wealthy are risk takers.

Does that mean you will never fail? Absolutely not. The wealthy have failed hundreds of times more than you and me. That is why they are wealthy.

*The wealthy know that failing does not make
you a failure. Never trying does.*

Robert Kiyosaki, best-selling author of *Rich Dad Poor Dad*, said that nine out of ten businesses fail. We hear that and say that means the odds are stacked against us. We should stay away from that. We say, "I have a 90% chance that I will fail."

The wealthy person says, "I have a 100% chance that I will succeed. I only have to start ten businesses to be a success."

It didn't matter that you failed on your first nine business ventures because on the tenth, you made ten million dollars.

Very few people have failed as many times as Donald Trump, yet he is far from being a failure.

We see risks as something we can't afford to take. The wealthy see risks as something they can't afford not to take.

For the last ten years of my life, I was just like the rest of the body of Christ. I was waiting for something to fall down on me, hoping the job would give me a raise. But it didn't matter how much money I made, at the end of the month, like everybody in America, I had the same amount left over. As I began to step out and think differently this past year, my life began to change.

Last year I thought I was taking a huge risk by getting into a million dollar project. One year later, I had over $13 million worth of projects. What happened is that I started to think like a billionaire. I used to say I can't afford to do that. Now I say I can't afford not to.

One of my partners spoke to me a few months into this process. He is a very intelligent man, a financial mentor of mine. He said, "We need to buy more."

"Whoa," I responded, "hold on Daddy Warbucks. We already have three million going. That is enough."

He said, "There is a window of opportunity, and life is all about windows. Windows of opportunity open up for a brief period and then they are gone. If we don't step into those windows of opportunity, we will miss them."

If I hadn't stepped in last year where I stepped in, I would have missed the opportunity to make an amazing amount of money in real estate. I would have just held on to one investment. I would have made some money but by stepping out, I have made a tremendous amount.

Wisdom

It is amazing to me that the wealthy think differently about the wisdom found in books and tapes and CDs. The average American reads one book a year and I am not talking love stories or *People Magazine*. I am talking about a self-help motivating book.

The wealthy read an average of two books a week. I read somewhere that Donald Trump reads two books a week—and he's got billions of dollars.

> **The wealthy know that wisdom is a key to abundance.**

The wealthy know that wisdom is a key to abundance. They have a burning desire for more information on every area of investing from real estate to stocks to business. They constantly want more information on investing. The rich don't waste their time listening to mindless radio in their cars. Instead they say, "That's an hour a day, five hours a week, twenty-five hours a month, 300 hours a year, 15,000 hours in a lifetime (equivalent to twenty-four hours a day for two years straight) that I could spend listening to tapes and CDs that could benefit my life." Radio is not doing anything for their lives, but these tapes and CDs are getting them the wisdom that sets them thinking differently, which then gets them producing differently in their lives.

What is amazing is that since I have been listening to tapes and CDs, I have the exact same amount of time in my life for doing the things I was doing before. I just gave up the one hour of mindless listening to music. I don't even miss that hour. Now when I get out of the car, I feel different. I feel changed. I feel like I have done something with my day and it hasn't even started.

We think that self-help books are a last resort to fixing the problem. The wealthy see them as the start to not having a problem.

Time

The wealthy have a whole different way of thinking about time. We just pass the time away. We waste time. We let others steal our time. To the wealthy, time is their most valuable asset. We think money is the most valuable thing. The wealthy say, "I can get more money but I can never get more time."

To the wealthy, time is an irreplaceable resource. It is the only limited resource they have. You can replace everything in life except for your time.

You can steal the wealthy person's money. "No big deal. I can get more money."

You can take his possessions. "I can get more possessions."

The wealthy will not allow you to ever steal their time. Because time is something they can never replace.

We go through life allowing people to steal our time. We do things in our own lives that waste our time. I'm not talking about taking vacations or having hobbies, things that you do to relax. There's nothing wrong with unwinding by watching a football game. Those things are vital tools to recharge you and keep your mind fresh. As you will see, however, we do things that add no benefit to our lives whatsoever. Time is the thing we think we have so much of so we give it away, throw it away.

Once again, to the wealthy, time is the most valuable thing they have. They remove time wasters from their lives. They stop doing things that waste their time.

Here is an example where we all live. How many times in your life have you heard or said, "Look at that guy with his gardener taking care of his lawn and his maid cleaning the house. If I had that kind of money, I wouldn't waste it on that. I would give that money to the poor." It is that kind of thinking that keeps you from having that money.

The wealthy say, "With the time I save not doing my own lawn, I can make thousands of dollars. The time I save not cleaning my house, I can use to make millions over my lifetime. I am also giving into a business, giving that business the opportunity to invest and get to where I am."

We spend twenty hours of frustration and $500 at Home Depot to paint the inside of our house by ourselves.

When we get done, it looks like an amateur did it. If we paid someone a thousand dollars to do it and took that time and invested it, we would be so much further ahead.

We have a "just-get-by" attitude rather than seeing time the way the wealthy see it. Those twenty hours I would spend painting are way too valuable to me. To be able to buy twenty hours of time for $500 is one of the best deals I ever made.

I used to battle it out with my pool every week, spending $30 or more a month on chemicals. Now, for $70 a month, I have someone clean my pool for me. For $40 a month, I bought five hours of time. I used to spend two hours a week doing my lawn. Now, for $150 a month, my lawn is done for me. I bought eight hours of time for $150. I then use that time researching, looking at and giving into my investments. In the last year, my greatest investments were the ones I put into my time.

Summing It Up

We have to change our entire mind-set. If we can change how we think, we will change our lives. If we can think as the billionaires, we begin to change everything in our lives and all of a sudden, abundance just naturally flows out into our lives just like it does into Trump's life.

Take this journey with me. I guarantee that in one year, if you change your thinking, you will dramatically change your life.

Be sure to visit LifeWithScot.com for bonus video teachings that are designed to accompany this chapter.

2
THINKING DIFFERENTLY ABOUT MONEY

*A*s he thinks in his heart, so is he...
-Proverbs 23:7

Let's start first by changing how we think about money. The first thought process we must tackle is the thought that it is spiritual to be poor, the thought that Christians should not have abundance. I know people can pull scripture out of context and talk about how we should be poor. But I can show you so many scriptures that say God wants you to have abundance. I ask that you use common sense when reading the Bible. What type of father does not want his children to be blessed? What type of father does not want his children to have abundance in their lives? What type of father does not want his children to be successful? Understand that the key to being a Christian and having abundance is the attitude of the heart.

Most Christians remain in the "just-get-by" state because deep down in places they don't even know exist, they have a misconception that it is spiritual to be poor. It is this battle within you that keeps you in lack. You want abundance, want to change, but as you think, so are you.

Until you change this area of thinking, you will be stuck just getting by.

The biggest problem that holds Christians back, that holds the Church back from doing so much more, the problem that keeps the wealth of the wicked in the hands of the wicked, is this thought that has been passed down from generation to generation. It is the thought that it is spiritual to be poor.

Whether we believe it consciously or subconsciously, somewhere, deeply rooted in some of the old religions, some of the things the media has said, even in the thinking of the world, is the belief that if you are a Christian, then you should be poor. We have this thing inside of us and if we can't change that foundation of our thoughts, if we can't get that thinking out, then we will never step into abundance. Where you are inside is where you're going to be outside because deep down, you think it's kind of spiritual to be poor. It's kind of spiritual to not have that much, just getting by. Until you can break that one thought, you will never be able to step into the abundance that God wants you to have.

I was recently in Rome and visited Vatican City. This facility is worth trillions of dollars, yet it sends out the message that it is spiritual to be poor. It contains millions of square feet, yet the Pope, the biggest religious leader of the day, lives in a humble 800-square foot apartment.

I told my dad, "Make me Pope. I will change the world by changing just two things. One, the Pope is getting married. I'm no good leading the church with all this testosterone flowing throw my veins. Number two, I'm taking over one of these buildings as my home." All of a sudden, the message that it is all right to have abundance, that being poor isn't spiritual, will begin to permeate the body of Christ. All of a sudden you will have Christians out getting the wealth that was laid up for them. All of sudden it will be a benefit to be a Christian, not a burden. In two acts, I could literally change the world, this generation, and many generations to come.

*T*o *be able to give away riches is mandatory if you wish to posses them. This is the only way that you will be truly rich.*

-Muhammad Ali

From cover to cover, the Bible is all about being blessed so that we can be a blessing. Look at how Paul said it.

For you know the grace of our Lord Jesus Christ, that though He was rich, yet for your sakes He became poor, that you through His poverty might become rich. *(2 Corinthians 8:9)*

And he continues in the next chapter.

And God is able to make all grace abound toward you, that you, always having all sufficiency in all things, may have an abundance for every good work. *(2 Corinthians 9:8)*

If I have just enough, God is unable to say, "Hey, give over here, give over there." I can't give out of my lack. But if I have this abundance He is talking about, I can give for every good work.

Right now, if you heard they needed Bibles in India, you could do something. Most of us can give a few hundred dollars. Imagine if you could say, "How many Bibles do you need? Will a million do?" You have positioned yourself to be a blessing. You are blessed to be a blessing.

In Genesis 12:2-3, God said, "I will make you a mighty nation. I will make you abundant. I am going to make you blessed so that you can be a blessing." That is God's plan.

Deuteronomy 8:18 says God gives you power to get wealth. Now why would God give you the power to get wealth, tell you that He gave you the power, and then get mad at you for using the power? That doesn't make any sense at all. God gave you the power. He wants you to use the power so that you can be blessed to be a blessing. But under the mind-set that it is spiritual to be poor and not to be blessed, we are limited in what we can do for the body of Christ.

On Saturday morning, I like to sleep in a little bit. So I have given my eleven-year-old and nine-year-old the power to obtain breakfast. I have given them the resources. I have shown them how and I have given them all that they need so they have the power to obtain the breakfast. Would it make any sense if I got up on Saturday, came downstairs and got angry with them because they made their own breakfast? I gave them the power to obtain their breakfast. I told them about it and even showed them how. I would be a horrible father if I got mad at them for doing what I told them they could do.

Following the same example, we see the mindset of the Christian community today. What if I came down the steps and my children were crying out, "Father, Abba, Father, why have

> **God gave you the power. He wants you to use the power.**

you forsaken us? We have been crying out all morning for the breakfast, yet you would not give us the breakfast. We have called out to you in the name of the Son, we had faith, yet you did not provide the breakfast for us, Father. Why have you forsaken us?"

Well, I haven't forsaken them. I have given them the resources for the breakfast. I have told them that you can do it. I have even showed them how, but they have to go and make their own breakfast.

God has given everyone reading this book the opportunity and the resources for great wealth. We live in America where we have the greatest opportunity that the world has ever known for wealth and abundance. All God is saying is, "Go get it."

The Bible says the wealth of the wicked is laid up for the just. Number one, He wouldn't lay it up for us if He didn't want us to have it. Two, it is laid up. The Bible doesn't say it is given to the just in a way that it falls down from heaven into the laps of the just. It says it is "laid up," meaning we have to go get it. It is time Christians went out and got what is rightfully theirs. It is time we got the money from the world and started using it the way God intended, to be a blessing on all occasions.

Let them shout for joy and be glad,
Who favor my righteous cause;
And let them say continually,
"Let the LORD be magnified,
Who has pleasure in the prosperity of His servant."
                                                    (Psalm 35:27)

What a sick God we would serve if He took pleasure in our prosperity and then was angry at us for having it. This verse says God takes pleasure, but let's not overlook the part right before that because it is the key. Understand that our prosperity is to magnify the Lord. Or in other words, it is to make God look bigger to the world.

The world, whether you know it or not, is watching you. Your neighbors know that you're a Christian whether you told them or not. They know on Sundays whether you go to church or not. They are looking at your life. They are looking at your marriage. They are looking at your children. They are looking at your finances. They are watching to see if life is different when you are a Christian.

When they look at you and you are just as broken down as they are and you don't have anything and your marriage is falling apart and your kids are having just as much trouble as theirs, they say, "Why in the world would I want to be a Christian?" But if they can look at you and me and they say, "Why do you have such an amazing life? Why do you have such a great marriage? Your children actually listen to you. You seem to have an abundance in every area of life. We make the same amount of money and you have so much more in your life. What do you have that we don't have?" and we are able to say, "We have Jesus Christ," right then you have just made God bigger. You have just magnified Him to the world. You did more for the body of Christ than if you stood on the street corner and preached damnation for fifty years. Your abundant life will get more people saved than a million "You're going to hell! Burn, baby, burn" tracks.

If you are a salesman and you get all the good deals and everything seems to go your way, you just say, "I've got Jesus Christ." You have just made God bigger. Understand that your job as a Christian is to make God bigger.

I want the world to look into our lives and say, "That is an amazing God that they serve, Who has pleasure in the prosperity of His servants."

But you say that you know some people who got money and it ruined them. Under that same thinking, I know people who got married and it ruined them, and so are we supposed to say that marriage is evil? I know people who got into church and it ruined them. Does that make church evil?

Money is not good or evil. Money is amoral. That means it doesn't have the power to be good or evil. It is incapable of being good or evil. It is what we do with the money that makes it good or evil. It is up to you whether or not the money is used to do good or evil.

Is a baseball bat good or evil? Well, if you take your kids out and play some baseball with them, the bat is good. If, in an angry rage, you bust your neighbor's car up, then it is evil.

Is a hundred dollar bill good or evil? Well, if you take that money and take the family out for a great night of relationship building, I would say that money is good. If you take that money and pay for a hooker, that money is evil. The money is not inherently good or evil. It matters what you do with it. If you get an abundance and you are a blessing with it, then the money is good.

I was reading an article about Bill Gates the other day in the newspaper. Bill Gates devoted a billion dollars a couple of years ago to medical research. Was the money good or bad? He used the money for good, so the money that he had was good.

I don't know if Bill Gates is a Christian or not but it should be the body of Christ making the news. It should be the body of Christ that the world is looking at. It should be us who are giving billions of dollars. Hurricane Katrina happens and the whole world turns to the church and we say, "We got it. How much do you need? Will $100 billion do? Do you need more? Just let us know. We will magnify God by being a blessing. Who do we make the check out to? We can handle it because we are so blessed."

"You need Bibles over in India? Okay, we got it covered. How much do you need me to write a check for?"

Imagine what you could do with the $60 billion that

Bill Gates has. You could pay off every single church debt in America. You could provide Bibles for everyone in the world. Imagine what the body of Christ could do if we controlled the wealth. We could do what we were called to do: change the world.

The problem is that Satan has us working for the money. You have to work forty, fifty, sixty hours a week for the money. Now, imagine your money working for you. Now you have forty, fifty, sixty hours to give into the kingdom, to be a blessing. That is time that can go towards your destiny.

Most people don't get into their God-given purpose, not because they don't want to, not because they don't have a desire to, but because they have to spend all their time and energy working for their money. If we follow God's plan, we can get to the place where we say, "Okay, church, I've got forty hours. What do you need me to do? I can help out and do whatever you need because I have the money working for me."

> **The world doesn't know what to do with money.**

The world doesn't know what to do with money. They waste it on drugs and alcohol and a myriad of other things, trying to find some peace, trying to find some happiness. The Bible asks, what good is it to gain the whole world but lose your soul? You lose your ability to be happy. The Bible says God gave them the desires of their hearts but sent leanness to their souls. They lost the ability to be happy. You can get rich the world's way. People do it all the time. But it's not worth it.

This book is about gaining wealth God's way. God's way is to have a heart and attitude of giving. We are blessed so we can be a blessing on all occasions. In a sense, I get my cake and I eat it, too, because I have abundance. But more importantly, I also have happiness, peace and joy.

The world is confused about what to do with their money. It makes me laugh when I see big Hollywood concerts held to raise money for AIDS or some other charity. They get a hundred musicians together (who are just doing it for positive publicity) and they do a big concert and raise $300,000. I watch this, thinking, *You made over $15 million last year. If you just gave your tithe of $1.5 million, we would have five times the money and wouldn't have to watch your stupid concert. We wouldn't have to listen to how concerned you are. If you're concerned, give out of your abundance.* Imagine if each artist at the concert gave, and each producer and each movie star. They could hand over a check for $30 billion. That would take care of a lot of AIDS research. But the world doesn't know what to do with its money.

The younger generation is looking to the Brad Pitts and saying, "I want to be like Brad Pitt," and, "I want to be like Julia Roberts." My goal in my generation is for the body of Christ to get to the place where the younger generation wants to be like us. They say, "I want to be like that man of God. I want to be like that woman of God." I want a new television show. Instead of the *Lifestyles of the Rich and Famous*, I want the *Lifestyles of the Rich and Chris-*

tian. Now that's a television show where we are blessed and we are pouring out the blessings.

You are called to be blessed so you can be a blessing. It is time we got rid of the idea that religious poverty is spiritual thinking. Begin to think the way God thinks and step into the abundance He wants you to have. It is time we allow Him to take pleasure in our prosperity. It is time the body of Christ got back that which the devil stole. It is time we got that wealth and used it to glorify and magnify God. It is time the world looked at us and said, "I want to be a part of that."

We make a living by what we get, but we make a life by what we give.

-Winston Churchill

Be sure to visit LifeWithScot.com for bonus video teachings that are designed to accompany this chapter.

3
SEEKING WISDOM

In seeking wisdom thou art wise; in imagining that thou hast attained it - thou art a fool.

-Lord Chesterfield

Understand that this chapter is probably the most important part of the book. Without this chapter, the rest will not do much for you. This is a chapter you need to read through as many times as it takes to get it. This chapter changed my life, and if you allow it to, it will change yours.

What is it that everyone deep down wants? What is it that every human being desires? I don't care where you are at. You could be in New York. You could be in Ethiopia. You could be anywhere in the world. Deep down, we have the same wants and desires. Everyone wants peace, joy and to have a sense of fulfillment. They want a long life, a healthy life and a little bit of money. Deep down, this is what everybody wants in life.

Here we are trying to get money. We spend all our time going after money. But God says, "Don't look for that." In Proverbs 3, He says to get wisdom and understanding. Then the desires of your heart will come.

Happy is the man who finds wisdom,
And the man who gains understanding;
For her proceeds are better than the profits of silver,
And her gain than fine gold.
She is more precious than rubies,
And all the things you may desire cannot com-
        pare with her.
Length of days is in her right hand,
In her left hand riches and honor.
Her ways are ways of pleasantness,
And all her paths are peace.
She is a tree of life to those who take hold of her,
And happy are all who retain her.
                    (Proverbs 3:13-18)

Wisdom and understanding will bring all the desires of your heart. Jesus said fifteen times in the New Testament, "Hear and understand." Every time He spoke one of His big parables, He said, "I need you to hear this but I need you to understand."

The understand part is what this chapter is all about. It is one thing to hear. It is so much more to understand. Hearing changes nothing. Understanding brings direction and action to our lives.

We hear so many things in a given week, but it is only the things we understand that cause us to take action. Every Sunday, we hear so many different teachings but we are not understanding. How do I know? Because nothing changed in our lives. We have heard so many teachings on financial abundance, yet we have not understood one of them. How do I know? Because nothing changed.

Understanding is a producer. It always causes us to take action. When I understand something, it will change my life.

A man goes to a marriage seminar and he hears how to treat his wife but he doesn't understand it. If he understood it, he would begin to treat her like she was the most valuable thing in his life, taking her out, learning how to communicate with her, buying flowers and loving her unconditionally. But instead, he goes home and does the same old things and wonders why he has the same old marriage. He heard but did not understand.

Let's look at an incident in the life of Jesus. Most call this a miracle. I call it a moment of understanding. We have all heard this story many times. The interesting thing is how most pastors miss the real meaning of this story. This story isn't about getting the miracle. It is about getting understanding. It is found in Luke.

So it was, as the multitude pressed about Him to hear the word of God, that He stood by the Lake of Gennesaret, and saw two boats standing by the lake, but the fishermen had gone from them and were washing their nets. (Luke 5:1-2)

Verse three is the most important part of the story.

Then He got into one of the boats, which was Simon's, and asked him to put out a little from the

land. And He sat down and taught the multitudes
from the boat.   *(Luke 5:3)*

Why teach first? Why didn't Jesus just tell Peter to cast his nets to the other side, get some fish, have a fish fry and get a pat on his miracle-working back?

Let's stop reading the Bible like it is some story. Instead, put yourself in Simon's shoes. You have been fishing all night and got nothing. You're tired. You know there are no fish in this stupid lake.

If Jesus just walked up and said to cast your nets to the other side, you would have said, "Sorry, Mr. Winemaker, I'm going home. I'm tired." You would have heard His words, but would not have understood them. Because of that, you would not have taken the action.

Jesus knew this was how the fishermen would react, so He said, "I have to first get them to understand. Then I can ask for the action." So He taught them first.

When He had stopped speaking, He said to Simon,
"Launch out into the deep and let down your nets
for a catch."
But Simon answered and said to Him, "Master, we
have toiled all night and caught nothing; never-
theless at Your word I will let down the net."
And when they had done this, they caught a great
number of fish, and their net was breaking.
                                              (Luke 5:4-6)

The abundance came into their lives when they understood. The understanding brought action. Peter may have been a little skeptical at first but because of what he had just learned, he decided to step out into the unknown.

My question is, did Jesus make the fish appear at that moment? No, the fish were always there. The abundance, the miracle was always available. It wasn't until they understood that they could step out, take a risk, and get the abundance that God had for them that they saw the miracle work for them.

You are sitting in a lake of limitless opportunity.

I want everyone reading this book to know that the abundance in life is already around you. It is all over. There are so many investment opportunities, so many different stocks. There is so much potential out there for businesses to be started. You are sitting in a lake of limitless opportunity.

For years we have been toiling, working hard, trying to get the wealth. But as you will see, we don't understand. Once we get the understanding of the principles in our hearts, it allows us to begin to put our nets where the miracles and abundance are waiting.

God has been speaking to you. He's been saying, "Do this investment. Buy this property." But when we don't understand, we don't act.

How many pieces of property have you driven up to and said, "I could have bought that land years ago for this amount. Look at it today. It's worth ten times that. I knew I should have bought it."

Why didn't you? You didn't understand. Everybody reading this book has had that happen. There was a moment years ago when God said to you, "Cast your net." You heard it but you did not understand it, and because you did not understand it you could not step out.

If you talk to a man in a language he understands, that goes to his head. If you talk to him in his language, that goes to his heart.

-Nelson Mandela

When we went to Europe, we were at a big pastors conference. Everybody in France obviously speaks French. My French is somewhat limited. I know French fries, French poodle, French kiss—and that's about it. This limits me to a great degree while I am in France. My lack of understanding limits my life.

Now every restaurant we visited had the menu printed in French only—and a waiter whose English was about as broad as my French. After seven days, my goal became being able to order something other than spaghetti. I wanted something that came from a cow. One more round of spaghetti and someone was going to get a French-style butt whipping. The problem was that the only thing I understood on the stupid menu was spaghetti and I love to eat so much that I don't want to risk the chance that I would get something that I didn't want. So I just continued to eat spaghetti.

On the menu was the opportunity to have all the food my little heart desired, but the problem was that I do not understand the French language. I could not tap into the full potential. I was limited not by what I heard, because the waiter told me all the specials—in French. I was limited by my understanding.

In the menu of life, we have the opportunity to order all we desire. God wants us to have the desires of our hearts. We have the opportunity to order the abundance, but since we don't have understanding, we continue to order the spaghetti of life and we continue to stay right in the exact same place. We are sick of the spaghetti of life but we don't want to risk getting something we don't like.

But suppose I begin to learn French. I have opened up a whole new world of ordering. If we can begin to learn the language of the wealthy, if we can understand what the rich speak, we can begin to order what they order.

In France, there could be hundreds of people around me speaking French but my mind blocks it out because I don't understand it. Your mind will always block out that which it does not understand.

One day, while doing the tourist thing, my bladder let me know we had roughly two minutes to empty it or it was going to take matters into its own hands. I went into place after place trying to find a bathroom. I asked. They replied in French. I had no clue what they were saying. I moved on. My mind blocked it out.

Your mind blocks out all these opportunities in your life. You are hearing investment opportunities all the time as you are walking and Jesus says, "Cast your net over here." But you continue to block it out because it's French to you. All the while, the wealthy, who have learned the language, continue to step out and continue to make money.

Ten years ago, you knew you should have bought that land. Seven years ago, you said, "Look how much it went up. I should have bought it three years ago." Then five years ago, you saw the same piece of land and you said, "Look how much it went up. I should have bought it two years ago." And then today, you saw the same piece of land and said, "I should have bought it five years ago."

There has to come a point when you understand and you say, "If I buy it today, if I throw my net over today, in two years, I won't be able to say that anymore."

How many invention ideas have you had? "Man, I had that idea. I should be the millionaire." The reason you're not is because you don't speak the language. You don't understand. So you never step out. You are hearing of so many opportunities, but until you learn the language and start to understand it, you will never step out into abundance.

In the late 80s, one of my college teachers said, "Buy Microsoft."

I said, "I am only making $3.35 an hour."

He said, "Take whatever you can and buy it."

I don't think anyone in the class took notice of his words. If I had been buying Microsoft at $10 or $20 a week back then, I would be worth millions of dollars today. I heard, but I did not understand.

We look at most of the wealthy people out there and we think they made most of their money on land and we think, "Man, are they lucky." It never clicks. We never see the light bulb go on and say, "Maybe I should look into that."

As I said, I read book after book and listened to hundreds of hours of CDs. I did it primarily to put together a teaching series for my church. As I got all of this in me, all of a sudden I started to understand some of the things I was hearing.

> **Rather than seeing how much I lost, I saw how much this other person gained.**

I remember the first piece of property I bought. I looked at it and I remembered looking at the exact same piece a few years back.

I asked the realtor how much it was and he told me $225,000. I said, "You mean pesos, right? Because two years ago I could buy this thing for $100,000." I said, "No thanks."

As I was getting in the car, it clicked. All of a sudden, all that information I had been studying, all those CDs, took hold. All of a sudden, I started understanding the language of the wealthy.

Rather than seeing how much I lost, I saw how much this other person gained. If I bought this land today, how much would it be worth next year? I said, "Let's buy it." Two months later, I sold it for $300,000. And that catapulted me into where I am today.

It's like learning French. How do I learn French? I have to listen to the tapes and read the books and I've got to study it and study it. I keep doing this long enough and, all of a sudden, I begin to understand French.

The rich speak a language we do not understand. So we continue to block it out. We continue to pack up our fishing gear and go home, missing our miracles of abundance. We speak the language of "just enough." We speak the language of average. It is what our parents spoke. Isn't that where we learned our language? You grew up learning to just get a job and get by. Don't take risks. Just work your job.

It is time we begin to speak the language of "too much," the language of "live a destiny and a dream." It is time we learn the language so we can begin to order all of our hopes and dreams from the menu of life.

The rest of this book is to help you learn the language of the wealthy. Think of it as a language lesson. Learn it, and then begin to cast your nets on the other side.

*N*o *man was ever wise by chance.*
                    -Lucius Annaeus Seneca

Be sure to visit LifeWithScot.com for bonus video teachings that are designed to accompany this chapter.

4
VISION: A DIFFERENT WAY
TO THINK ABOUT MONEY

*I*t is a terrible thing to see and have no vision.
                                        -Helen Keller

We live in a world of now. I have been trained to get what I want, when I want, how I want, and I want it all now. I get to have it all my way. Why wait? Why save? Charge it. Finance it. Can't afford it? No big deal. Finance that puppy for a lifetime. My kids will be paying on it.

There is one distinct difference in thinking between the wealthy and the rest of us. When it concerns money, the wealthy have self-control. This is one of the biggest battles you have to win on the inside of you. Without control of yourself, the rest of this book will be useless. We will be discussing the thought process inside of you that needs to change, that can bring self-control into your life. At the end of the book is a workbook you need to begin going through. This workbook was a key part of my financial success.

To have self-control, you need vision.

Where there is no revelation, the people cast off restraint.   (Proverbs 29:18)

Vision brings restraints and boundaries into your life. Without vision you have no boundaries.

I was twelve years old and there was this new video game coming out in two weeks that I wanted. I asked my dad to loan me the $30. He said, "No, son, you need to save your money."

At this time in my life, I did not possess the skill of saving. I had zero dollars in the piggy bank. But vision for that game got in my heart. I had two weeks to save $30. I only got $2 a week allowance, so that meant I was fifteen weeks away from having $30.

I got to thinking. My dad gave me $2 a day for lunch and even though eating was something I loved to do, that vision wouldn't allow me to eat. I had just found $20, plus my $4 allowance for two weeks. That made $24. I worked after school doing extra jobs for Dad around the house every night and he gave me $6. That vision brought restraints into my life. It wouldn't allow me to eat lunch or spend money. I had gained self-control.

You have probably had a similar experience. You had no money saving skills whatsoever, but you needed a down payment for a house. For the last five years you hadn't saved a dime, but in six months, you were able to save thousands. What happened? You got vision in your heart. That vision brought self-control.

What gets a marathon runner to run ten miles a day? Vision. What gets a gymnast to practice eight hours a day? Vision. What gets a person headed for wealth to not buy the perks in life and to invest instead? VISION!

You see, the wealthy don't have more self-control than we do. What they do have is a vision. This chapter is about putting vision in your heart, and then keeping the flames of vision hot until you get to your destination.

That last part is probably the most important—keeping the flames hot. I think we all have read a book or heard a seminar on finance and left with a vision in our hearts. We took off running towards wealth. That vision lasted almost a month and then we settled right back into the old ways. The workbook helped me keep the vision hot, keep it going. The workbook kept restraints in my life.

> **You got a vision in your heart. That vision brought self-control.**

*G*ood business leaders create a vision, articulate the vision, passionately own the vision, and relentlessly drive it to completion.

-Jack Welch

Understand that your mind takes you to where your vision wants to go. Your mind will not allow you to sabotage that which is in your heart, so when you are standing in front of something you want that costs $200, you will be able to say, "NO!" You know that $200 invested properly can net hundreds of thousands of dollars, so instead of doing what feels good by buying that item, you keep the money and invest it for your future, which is the right thing to do.

Habakkuk 2:2 says, "Write the vision and make it plain on tablets." In other words, let's write our vision down—but keep it simple. It is the simplicity of this that will keep those flames of vision hot.

This workbook needs to be your best buddy and it should go wherever you go. Anytime you start to waiver in self-control, anytime you get discouraged, take it out and fan those flames of vision. What happens when you fan a fire that is almost out? It gets hotter than it was before. I will say this one more time. This workbook is what pushed me into success. In this workbook are all the tricks I learned from the rich, all the things they used to change their thinking.

The workbook starts out detailing when the vision was birthed. I hope that will be today. Write that down.

Next is a key scripture that kept me going no matter what things looked like. Remember, you change your thoughts by getting new thoughts. A great way to do this is through confession. Faith, or believing something can happen, comes by hearing—hearing God's Word.

For whatever is born of God overcomes the world.
(1 John 5:4)

On your journey, you will have people and circumstances say your vision will never happen. You should give up. It is too big of a risk. All you need to do is open your workbook and say, "For whatever is born of God overcomes the world." You need to know that this is born of God so whatever problems or obstacles come will be removed because the vision that God has given to you will overcome the world.

The first part of our vision is our heart, which is the vision of giving. The Bible says if you build His house, He will build your house. The priority that we have inside of us for attaining millions and billions is that in our hearts, we want to build God's house. He is our Source, He is our Daddy, and He's the One. We know that if we build His house, then He will build our houses.

Our heart in this program is to be blessed to be a blessing. To obtain wealth God's way, we have to start out with an attitude of giving. If we want to employ God in this, then we need to have a heart for Him. You can become wealthy on your own. It is more work and as the Bible says, it comes with sorrow. Proverbs 10:22 says, "The blessing of the LORD makes one rich, and He adds no sorrow with it."

The world has the money but they need a drink to get them going. They need an upper to keep them up and a downer to let them sleep. They need another sexual conquest. They have the riches but there is sorrow with it. When we do things God's way, we get the blessings and we have the peace, joy, happiness, and fulfillment God wants us to have. When your heart is one of giving, God says, "Let Me help."

You might say, "Well, I will give when I have money." God knows that if you won't give a hundred dollars, there is no way you will ever give a hundred thousand.

But if you are faithful in the little, He will make you ruler over much.

We start with the tithe. What is your vision for the tithe? I wanted to give $100,000 a year. I will do that this year. Write down the annual tithe that you want to be giving. Now write out a check for that amount and place it over the appropriate spot in the workbook.

Next, it is time to write the vision for your offering. Your annual offering is over and above your tithe. Write out a check and place it where it says "offering" in the workbook. I have written a check out for a million dollars that I keep in my workbook. This is a goal of mine to write an offering for that amount. That is my vision.

This next part is about you. What is your net worth? What is your vision for your destination? Vision is about destination. Without a destination, you have no way of knowing if you are headed in the right direction. When I plan a vacation, I write a vision. This is where I am going.

Vision is all about finishing before you start. I finish my vacation. Then I can start it. Once the vision is finished, I know how to prepare for it. So let's finish your finances. Then we know where we are headed and what preparations we need to make to get there.

I wrote out that I personally want a billion dollars. The tithe on a billion dollars is $100 million a year. Imagine what I can do across America and in India with a hundred million dollars each year. That is my vision and I tell you to not stop short in your vision.

Don't sell yourself short on this part. You might

think you can live comfortably with a million dollars in the bank. Once again, see beyond you. See what you can do for the world around you if you had more. What holds most of us back from wealth is this thinking that says, "If I had a million dollars I'd go to Tahiti, relax and drink margaritas. That's all I would do."

Your vision dictates your outcome.

Tiger Woods has hundreds of millions of dollars. I hear people say that if they were Tiger Woods, they would just stop playing golf, relax and enjoy life. This is the reason why you and I aren't where he is today. There is a driving force, a vision inside of him, that won't allow him to settle in life.

God will take you to whatever you can envision. Make sure you do not sell yourself too short. "Well, I just want a business with a couple of employees, one that pays the bills." God says, "You could have done so much more, but here you go. You could have built a hundred-million dollar corporation, but if all you want is a get-by business, I can do that, too."

Your vision dictates your outcome. If your vision is big, your outcome will be big. If your vision is small, your outcome will be small. As you will see in this story, you dictate the size of the miracle.

In 2 Kings 4, we see the story of a woman who had bill collectors coming to her and threatening to take her children because she had nothing else left for them to take. Imagine that your life got so bad that you couldn't make your MasterCard payment, so they sent someone out to get little Johnny. "He's a hard worker. They could find some odd jobs for him to do."

It got that bad for this woman. So she went to Elisha and asked for help. He asked her what resources she had available. She answered that all she had was a little bit of oil. Elisha instructed her to round up all the containers, jars and pots she could find. He told her to borrow from the neighbors and anywhere she could find them. Then she was to start pouring the oil into the vessels she had collected.

She did as Elisha said and shut the door behind her. As she started pouring out the oil into other containers, it just kept coming. She and her sons kept at it until there were no more empty jars anywhere in the house. Then the oil stopped. (Remember that part. The oil stopped when the jars ran out.) They took the jars of oil and started selling them around town. When they were done, they had money to pay all of the bills and even extra that they could live on after that.

We can learn a lot from this story. First of all, you have to be willing to do something. The woman had to actually go out and get jars and then pour the oil into them. If you want to see God miraculously increase your finances, you have to give Him something to work with. He's not going to just pour money out of heaven on top of you. You have to do what you know how to do. Too many Christians fail to get a vision for great wealth beyond just dreaming. Having a vision means getting off your rear end and doing something so that God has something to bless.

In the New Testament, a little boy gave a couple of fish and some loaves of bread and with that, Jesus was able to feed five thousand people. But it started with the boy presenting what he had.

You have to give something in order for growth to take place. You will have to step out and give your time, energy and resources to make that business go, to get the land loan or investment property going.

The second thing we can learn is what I mentioned earlier. Make sure your vision is big enough. In the story, the woman ran out of vessels before she ran out of oil. God provided the amount of oil that she had a vision for. If she and her sons had grabbed twenty vessels, the oil would have filled twenty. If they had gathered thirty vessels, the oil would have filled thirty. The miracle did not dictate the size of the vision. Her vision dictated the size of the miracle.

We need to determine the size of our vision. If we decide to have a small mom and pop type of business, God will say, "Okay, we can do that." God will say the same thing when you have a vision for a multi-million dollar idea. But you have to have the vision first, a big vision that doesn't limit God.

Everything you achieve in life will require a vision first. If you can't see it, then you won't get it. You have to learn to think big. What if the woman had collected five more jars? She would have had five more vessels that would have been filled to the top. You need to change your expectations and think big. What can you do in your life on your own? That is as far as most people ever go. But God says, "Think bigger! Employ Me. Let Me be involved."

This is how I am thinking now.

I like thinking big. If you're going to be thinking anything, you might as well think big.

-Donald Trump

Understand that billionaires think big. Inside of them is a huge vision. They don't say, "Let's start a business that hopefully one day makes me $100,000 a year." A billionaire says, "Let's get a corporation going that makes billions of dollars a year." It is interesting that to the level we think, we produce.

We need to drive out that "just-get-by" attitude that says I just want enough so I can stop working and watch Oprah all day. No, I want enough so I magnify and glorify God on all occasions. I want to be, as the Bible says, a lender to nations. I will not stop short of being blessed to be a blessing on all occasions.

God does not want to be part of a plan that gets you money so you can do nothing. He will be a part of a vision that gets you to change the world around you.

Now that you have a vision for your net worth, now that you have written God a check, write yourself a check. I wrote one out for a million dollars to myself. I want it all in nickels. This is your vision and you need to write it out so you can go and cash it when you get there. What happens when you write your vision out? You open the workbook when things aren't going great in your life. Maybe it is a downer day so you open the book and a little spark gets going and you feel recharged and now you are not going to give up.

Now we come to our vision of gifts. These are the special gifts you would like to give to a ministry or to God—like a million Bibles sent over to India. These are gifts to build God's house. When you build God's house, God will build yours and you will have these things.

Delight yourself also in the LORD,
And He shall give you the desires of your heart.
                                        (Psalm 37:4)

Once again, we first gave to God. Now let's give to you. As long as you have a heart of giving, God takes pleasure in you enjoying some of the finer things in life. So now write out the desires of your heart. These are the things God (according to scripture) wants to give to you. These are the desires of your heart. We need to delight ourselves in God. As we go through the changing inside of us and we delight ourselves in God, He will be giving back.

> **God takes pleasure in you enjoying some of the finer things in life.**

A few weeks ago, my son, Baylor, went with his grandma for their "Grandma time," and she took him to get a special present. Baylor came home with this big Batman toy—the same toy that he had already gotten just two days earlier. I asked him why he got another one and he said, "Laken really liked mine, so I got this one for Laken." (Laken is his brother.)

As a father, this act of kindness touched my heart. At that moment I probably would have bought him anything his heart desired. A few days later, I took him out for a special day and I bought him a present twice as big as the one he picked because of his heart.

I believe when we have a heart like Baylor's, we inspire the same reaction with our Father God. When Baylor delights himself in my wishes, I want to bless him. I want to pour so much in his cup that he can't even contain all the ice cream and all of the goodies. And that is how God is with us. When we delight ourselves in Him, when we have the right attitude and the right heart, God says, "Okay, what are the desires? I'd love to give them to you. Here you go."

There is a place in the workbook for you to put pictures of those things you desire. We are a picture-oriented people. It will be these pictures that keep us pressing towards the vision of what we desire. I wanted a Hummer. I put a picture there, and wouldn't you know, three months later God blessed me with a Hummer. When I say blessed, I mean blessed. It has every option man could buy. God dropped it into my lap for the same price as my F150— $27,000. Yes, $27,000, and no, it isn't a salvage title. And it only had 22,000 miles.

An interesting thing is that God knows what we want before we ask. Most of the time we just need to ask. God knew I wanted a Hummer for the last five years but it wasn't until I asked that God said, "Here you go."

I want a plane so I have a picture of a plane. I know my destination. Why do I want a plane? Is it so I can get over to vacation quicker than everyone else? No, I want a plane so I can get around and I don't have to stand in line at the airport and I can minister and preach all over America. My own plane helps me guard my most valuable asset, my time.

There are certain things that I want to have and a lot of them are tied to my vision and purpose. There is nothing wrong with wanting things in life as long as your heart is right. My attitude and heart is that I want to be a blessing. When we delight ourselves in God, He says He wants us to have the desires of our hearts. That is why we have desires. Why do you think we want certain things in life? They're fun. Big screen and plasma TV's are fun. So put pictures of things like these that you want in your workbook. God wants you to have a plasma TV. He wants you to have a house that glorifies Him. He wants you to have the desires of your heart.

The size of your vision will determine the size of your harvest. If you have a vision for a small company with a few employees, then that is what you will produce. That vision is in your heart. If you can't see it, then you won't reach it because...

The lamp of the body is the eye. If therefore your eye is good, your whole body will be full of light. But if

your eye is bad, your whole body will be full of dark-
ness. If therefore the light that is in you is darkness,
how great is that darkness!

(*Matthew 6:22-23*)

What this scripture says is that what you see is what
you get. If you can see or envision it, you can have it. If
a man can dream it, it will happen. Whatever a man has a
vision for, he is able to do, no matter how many people tell
him he can't.

People said, "Man can't fly. Only birds can fly."
But a man had a vision and he found a way to fly. Everyone said there was no way you could ever send a man to the
moon, but a man with a vision made it happen.

If you doubt that it can happen, then you are right. If
you can see it happening, then you will do everything that
you need to do in order to make it happen. And God will
do the rest.

I have a big vision. I want a billion dollars so that I
can give away a hundred million dollars a year all over the
world. I want to be blessed so that I can bless others and
build churches all over. I want to be able to send Bibles or
write checks without even thinking about it. My vision is
so big that it's going to take God to do it. It's going to take
commitment on my part but it will also take a commitment
on God's part. I know that as long as I hold up my end of
the deal, God will take care of His.

It takes someone with a vision of the possibilities to attain new levels of experience. Someone with the courage to live his dreams.

                                        -Les Brown

Be sure to visit LifeWithScot.com for bonus video teachings that are designed to accompany this chapter.

5
COMMITMENT TO THE VISION

It is the nature of the wise to resist pleasures, but the foolish to be a slave to them.

-Epictetus

Now we move to the commitment. As James 1:8 reminds us, a double-minded man is unstable in all that he does. It may seem that no matter what you have tried in the past, you couldn't finish. You tried school and you were unstable. Why? Because you were not committed. You tried investing and quit. You tried real estate and you quit. Why? Because you were not fully committed.

To get to where your vision is, you have to be fully committed. If you aren't going to be committed to the whole process, don't even start. If you are committed, you will put your name down by your commitment in the workbook and date it.

Here is the commitment:

I am making a commitment to change what is in me, thus changing the life that is coming out of me. I will begin to think like a billionaire. I will begin to have God's thoughts so I can have

His ways. I will change what is in my heart so I
change what comes into my life. I am committed
to doing the things I list in my journal.

In this book, I am teaching the principles needed to
attain your vision. After each chapter, you will write the
principle down as a sign that you are committed to it. I
strongly urge you to take notes while reading this book.
Highlight the heck out of it. This is not a one-time reader.
You need to read this book over and over again until you
fully understand the language.

In the journal portion of the workbook, there is a
place at the bottom of the notes page for you to initial every single month to indicate you have been faithful to your
commitment. You might say, "Oh, I forgot about this investment." We forget about so many things and we wonder why we don't have everything working. We have to
continue to hear. Faith comes by hearing and hearing the
Word (Romans 10:17). The more we hear, the more faith
we have, the more confidence we have that we can step out
in all we want to do.

You are going to make commitment after commitment, working with the things you have committed to.
Let's list out the commitments we have made so far. One
is that we are committed to the thinking that God wants us
blessed. Two, we are committed to being blessed so we can
be a blessing. Three, we are committed to the vision we
placed in this book.

The next thing you are going to keep track of is your blessings. You are going to take time each week and write down your blessings. If you don't take time to write down your blessings, you forget about all of them and all of a sudden, problems come along and you get caught up in the problems. Billionaires have problems. We all have problems and that's what makes life what it is. Life is great but when we forget about the blessings we have had in our lives, we can let a mountain capture all of our thoughts.

Those problems build up faith and patience, and they get you to the place where you lack nothing.

You want to keep track of all the blessings and all of the things that God has given to you and take time to thank Him. You will enter His gates with thanksgiving and His courts with praise. Give God thanks and praise His name because He is so amazing. Praise and worship don't change God. He is the same yesterday, today and tomorrow. But praise and worship change you.

You have situations that come up. You have negative things going on in your life. When you praise God, it changes your attitude. Rather than being full of fear and worry, which holds you in the problem, you have an attitude of hope that helps you solve the problem. Thank God for your amazing life. Thank Him for your amazing children and thank Him for blessing your finances.

Your life is the same as it was before, but now you begin to think on those things that are pure, all those things that are good and holy, and you have an uplifted spirit and you can think more clearly (Philippians 4:8). Science has actually proven that people who can get rid of negative thoughts are able to solve problems or conquer things in their lives so much easier. It's almost as if God has opened a window in their minds and said, "Here you go."

If you can change your thought process about your problems and situations, you can live out James 1:2 that says to count it all joy when faced with problems. Those problems build up faith and patience, and they get you to the place where you lack nothing. How do you get to where you lack nothing? Problems.

This is where the next part of the workbook comes in—learning from your problems. This is the section on life lessons. Remember, the wealthy fail. What makes them different than us is that they learn and they don't stop trying. In this section, write down the life lessons of your own life—what you learned and what you will do next time. Review this monthly. You will be surprised how many repeat problems you avoid by doing this.

The next section of the workbook might just be the most powerful. Isaiah says if you get God's thoughts, you get His ways. Romans 12:2 says if we renew our minds (think like Him), we will experience His perfect will. Where are His thoughts? His Word. How do I get them? By hearing and hearing and hearing and hearing them. Faith, or change in your thinking, comes by hearing the Word over and over again. Confess these scriptures every day, over and over again. Speak them until they are a part of you. I suggest you make a CD of you speaking these confessions and play them throughout the night. Get this Word in your subconscious. Now watch as this Word and the change in your thinking take you to where God wants you to be. IN HIS ABUNDANCE!

Finally, write out a vision for your present finances. It is the end of the month and you have the same thought. *Where did all the money go? I made more than I did last year, yet I never have extra. What is missing?*

Vision. You have no vision over your finances so, you have no boundaries.

Whoever has no rule over his own spirit
is like a city broken down, without walls.
(Proverbs 25:28)

You are like a broken down city with no walls. VISA and MasterCard can raid your life and there is nothing you can do about it. I know a lot of you are thinking, "I have a budget." Yes, you may have a budget, but you don't have a vision. Complete the vision for your finances in the back of the book as you read along.

Here is a sample budget for most Americans today. It would look a little bit like this.

Income:	$1,200
Rent:	$350
Electricity:	$50
Car and Insurance:	$300
Gas:	$100
Food:	$200
Expenses Total:	$1,000

Extra money: $200 a month

You see this and think, "Oh, my gosh. I have $200 extra that I can go out and buy some clothes with." You think you have an extra $150 to spend on a better car. Then you get a raise and you make $2,000 per month and you go through this kind of budget. Now you have $1,000 to spend so you get a bigger car and you buy a $500 coat and just keep spending.

So what happens when Christmas rolls around? Wait a second. You didn't plan for Christmas in your budget and now you have to come up with about $500. How do most of us do that? We swipe a credit card. Birthdays come up and we don't have any extra money so we charge it. We need a new tire on the car so we charge that, too. Valentines, anniversaries and schoolbooks are all things we do not plan ahead for. We spend all of our money so we swipe our card which is pulling 15-30% interest, which means we are spending tomorrow's money today plus paying a high price to do it.

It is imperative to move past a budget and begin to have a vision for your money.

Let's go through the vision. Number one is your income. If you don't have one, this book will be a hard battle. Without seed, you can't plant. The first thing you need to do is put the book down and go get a job.

Income and weekly take-home salary are multiplied by 4.333 because that is how many weeks there are in a month.

Expenses are your absolute monthly expenses and I will break them down for you.

Your tithe is the most important bill you have each month. In Malachi, it tells us that our tithe protects our stuff. Over a lifetime, Satan can cause you millions and millions of dollars of damage because your car broke down or the washing machine quit working or you got a flat tire. People come up to me and say, "You are lucky. This never happens to you." No, I'm not lucky. I'm a tither. God protects my stuff so Satan can't get in here and mess with it.

It is imperative to move past a budget and begin to have a vision for your money.

For many of us, Satan comes in and steals business deals and opportunities and things keep getting stolen but we can't figure out why. Why is that? Because we aren't tithing like we are supposed to. We can't have the, "If-I-had-some-money-maybe-I'd-tithe," mentality anymore. The central principle of this is a heart and attitude of giving and if we can't give God 10% now, then what makes us think that He wants to be employed in our business adventure? Our 10% is an absolute on our budget.

After our tithes, we have offerings. Offerings are, according to the Word, where God can really bless our investments. If we give $10, $20 or $50 over and above, God says that the money will be given back to us—ten, twenty, even one hundred fold return. Your offering is very important because it is your seed.

Ten percent of your monthly income is investment money. You have to make this a bill in your budget if you want to get millions of dollars. If you want to become wealthy, then you have to have seed to plant into the earth. That will be 10% of your income. If you make $2,000 a month, then $200 per month is what you are going to invest.

What makes this program unlike any other is you can make $7 an hour and become a millionaire. Yes, $28 a week invested can easily become millions of dollars.

Remember, God gives seed to the sower. That is the one who sows into the church and also the one who sows into investment. Do not be the guy who buries his money out of fear. That money will be given to the one who invests it. Remember, a wealthy person steps out. Don't hold on to it in fear of, "What if I lose my house? What if I lose my car? What if I go bankrupt?" Seventy-five percent of all billionaires have been bankrupt at least once because they are risk takers and they are willing to step out. They aren't just burying their money in a bank earning 1%. They are planting their money and seeing the harvest.

Most people don't have investing in their budget and if this is you, then you need to be happy with where you are now because you will remain there for the rest of your life. Whenever you get a raise, it will get spent. Raise after raise, you just spend the money instead of budgeting investment money.

Other things in your vision are house payments, automobiles, auto insurance, homeowner's fees, electricity, gas, cell phones, and medical and dental insurance. I have these and more items listed on this vision. You must have a vision for everything for the year. You should not miss anything so you know exactly how much money that you have to spend. This will give you boundaries. I know for Christmas, I'm going to spend $50 per person. Now I have a boundary to work within. I have a set amount of money to spend on clothes, another amount allocated for home up-grades and when that money is gone, it's gone.

At the end, add up your expenses and subtract them from your income. If you are in the negative, don't go, "Oh, well." I have met with people who said, "Yes, we tried your vision thing, but every time we did it, we came up negative so we just threw it away." So ignoring the problem is going to fix it? You need to go back and take some money from clothes and fun. Keep cutting back until the vision works. (Never cut from the tithe or your investments.) If it still doesn't work, that means you need more income. Get a second job. Understand that this will be just a season of your life. You won't be here long. But to get to the good life, you have to give up certain things now.

Do what you have to so later you can do what you want to. You will hear this quite a bit in this book. We want to do what feels good, not what is good. What feels right, not what is right. If you do right today, tomorrow you can do what feels right.

Write down on your commitment page that you are committed to the financial vision (budget).

God is waiting eagerly to respond with new strength to each little act of self-control, small disciplines of prayer, feeble searching after Him. And His children shall be filled if they will only hunger and thirst after what He offers.

-Richard Holloway

If I walked up to you and said, "I will give you $3 million to quit drinking soda," would you do it? If I said, "I will give you $6 million if you quit smoking," would you do it? I want to show you how quitting a bad habit in your life can produce millions of dollars. This isn't the meat of the book, more of an extra. If anything, this part of the book will give you more seed to sow, which will produce millions of dollars over your lifetime.

If you quit the habit and invest that money, it can literally produce millions of dollars. I call it self-control to millions of dollars.

Understand that this principle works with your budget (vision). Take the money from the bad habit and add it to the investment part of your vision.

If you drink three Cokes a day, which is what the average person does, it costs you $4. Seven days a week, that is $28, which doesn't sound like a whole lot of money, but look at a year and it is $1,456 a year just on Cokes. Invested, it comes to $1,601 after a year. (This is in simple investments. Who knows how much it would be if invested in real estate.) When you skip ahead to twenty years of investing that Coke money, you have $89,000 in the bank. In thirty years, it would be $257,000 and after forty years, you would have $692,000. In fifty-five years you would have almost $3 million in the bank. So at eighteen, you stop drinking, smoking and eating fast food. When you are seventy-three years old, you have $9 million in the bank. That does not include your 10% investment. That is just extra money.

I have people come up to me and say that they don't have money to invest. I say, "Give up your soda. Now you have money."

In the workbook, you can write down all of your $4-a-day habits. You multiply for ten years and get $25,000 in the bank. (It is interesting to think that if ten years ago you had stopped drinking soda,

> **If you quit the habit and invest that money, it can literally produce millions of dollars.**

which is destroying your body, you would have money to buy a new car with cash. If you had stopped four habits, you would have $100,000 to invest with right now.) You can follow it down as it accumulates over the years rapidly.

The average American has three bad habits. When I say bad, I mean something that you are addicted to that takes money out of your future. It could be Starbucks. It could be smoking or soda. It could be fast food. It could be 7,000 channels of cable. Everyone reading this book can come up with a minimum of $12 a day.

If you smoke a pack or two a day, drink three sodas daily, and eat fast food four times a week or drink Starbucks and you have three bad habits, in ten years it comes to almost $9 million.

What makes this chapter so fun is everybody has habits. What we don't realize is the world holds us back with these. They want to keep us off track. I have to have my Coke, my smokes. We feel this need for these things and not only is it destroying our bodies but it is stealing our future money.

We don't even see it. We say, "Oh it's just three bucks," but it is slowly stealing our ability to put seed into the ground so that God can bless us.

I made the workbook to help you get a vision because vision is what's going to give you self-control. Nothing else has gotten you to quit cigarettes but maybe if I walked up to you and told you I was going to give you $3 million to stop smoking, you would stop. How many people could stop drinking Coca-Cola for $3 million? I strongly feel like I could and that is the way we need to think about this.

Just imagine that someone is giving you $3 million for every bad habit you have. Maybe you have four bad habits. Now you have that extra money you can begin to invest and it will begin to multiply. When you get around $25,000 in the bank, it is amazing because now the bank will let you use their money. I was able to get zero-down loans for $1 million because I had $25,000 in the bank. Now that I have money in the bank, they say, "Okay, here is a couple of million. Go play." I'm playing with their money, not my money.

Once you reach that $25,000 in your account, the banks are suddenly willing to loan you large sums of money. Now you have an extra million that you can invest and get to that point you are striving for. Look at your notes on the addictions and habits in your life and add it up so you get your vision. You need to put this where you see it first thing in the morning. Put it on the fridge so when you go to grab a Coca-Cola, you see it and think, "Oh my, that's $12 million. There ain't no way I'm throwing that away."

If you invest in self-control and invest 10% of your income, then what happens? Even if you never get a raise and you are making $10 an hour, you need to take the 10%, which is $40 a week, and invest it in a simple investment. That equals 1.5 bad habits. And that's in simple investments, not including land. After fifty years, you would have $4.5 million in the bank. You add three bad habits to the equation and you have $13.5 million. It is

> **Just imagine that someone is giving you $3 million for every bad habit you have.**

amazing that taking the money from habits and investing it will create opportunity like that. It's all about numbers and as soon as you have $25,000 in the bank, that money starts working for you. Now you play with the bank's money and in just over ten years, you have acquired millions of dollars, making just $10 an hour. That is where we're headed so you have to get a vision for self-control.

On your commitment page, write down the bad habits you are committed to giving up.

Let me tell you the problem most of us face. It is in a simple statement that has become part of our everyday vocabulary: "It's only a few dollars, what's the big deal?"

Let's take just one dollar not wasted and look at it's potential. Potential is the key. Let's say I am holding an apple in my hand and I ask you how many apples I am holding. The answer to that question is dependent upon what I do with that apple. If I take the seeds from the apple and plant them, cultivate them, then that seed will produce thousands of apples, which if planted, will produce millions of apples, which planted will produce an infinite amount of apples. If I take that apple and eat it, well I had a moment of pleasure with it, and I got my one apple.

The apple's potential is dependent upon me. Sure it is just an apple, what is the big deal—in the same way it is just a dollar, what is the big deal. But let's see the dollars potential. If I can get a clear view of what a dollar can produce, this might make me think twice before I simply enjoy the quick pleasure of today.

One dollar invested over a lifetime (50 years) will produce $117. Lets talk about how many dollars that daily Starbucks is actually costing you. I know it is just $3, but it's potential is $351. Is the coffee worth that much? To my wife, probably. Having 1000 channels of cable that steals your time from you is only $79 a month. But it's potential is over $9200. Is cable worth ten grand a month? That purse only costs $250, but it is costing you over $25,000.

Wealthy people can see the potential of a dollar. That is why most self-made millionaires drove the $400 car and bought their clothes from some outlet store. They kept their pleasures of life to a bare minimum. They knew that every dollar wasted was a forest of potential.

This is something I have done my whole life and it drives my wife nuts. When we go out to any restaurant, we all get waters, "Just get them their own drink, we have the money," she mutters every time. Yes we have the money, but that would be an extra $10, or $1000 of potential money every meal. Let me say this. I do believe in enjoying life and making memories with the family. That is priceless and should be done on a regular basis. But if I can save a few thousand dollars of potential money every meal, then I do it. I'm not saying sacrifice memories or date nights with your spouse. I'm saying look into your day and find thousands of dollars of future money that you are wasting. Memories are usually not a waste, but pleasures you can forgo, those are.

If you cut back your cable bill from $79 a month to basic cable for $19 a month, you are saving $5000 a month. Rather than financing that $600 a month luxury car, drive a nice $200 a month car. That is almost $50,000 a month. Ordering reasonably off the menu can save you $1000 a month.

When you can see the potential of something, it changes what you do.

Be sure to visit LifeWithScot.com for bonus video teachings that are designed to accompany this chapter.

6

BILLIONAIRES PREPARE TODAY FOR THE OPPORTUNITIES OF TOMORROW

*B**y failing to prepare, you are preparing to fail.*
-Benjamin Franklin

B illionaires think differently about wisdom and under-standing. We get wisdom when we need it. Billion-aires get wisdom long before it is relevant in their lives. They read books on things they won't use for years. We don't read a book until we need the information today. They think differently so they produce much differently than the rest of us.

I was meeting with a guy who wanted to build and sell houses. He came to me and said, "I found some land. I have forty-five days to close."

I said, "Do you have financing in place? Do you have an architect? Do you have any drawings?"

He said, "No. That is what I'm doing here."

Needless to say, he wasn't able to close the deal and potentially lost a minimum of $300,000. Why? Because he was thinking like the rest of us. We prepare for today.

Billionaires prepare today for the opportunities of tomorrow. Billionaires prepare for tomorrow while the rest of us prepare for today. When opportunity presents itself to us, we aren't ready and we miss it. Billionaires know that life is about windows of opportunity. If they are not ready for the window, they will miss the opportunity. Every missed opportunity can cost you millions of dollars. Billionaires are constantly getting ready for what tomorrow may bring. As we begin to think like a billionaire, we start to think about tomorrow.

People have windows of opportunity open for them all the time, but they usually miss them because they are not prepared. The windows close before they take action. A business opportunity becomes available but they miss out. We've all done it. You had an invention that you never acted on and it is now a household product. You saw land for sale at a great price but you didn't get around to buying it. You saw a great deal but someone bought it before you could.

We think, "Why prepare for something that may never happen?" Think about Noah. He had a window open that he had prepared for, not really knowing what he was preparing for. What if he said, "I'm not going to build an ark. What if I spend all this time building this ark and it doesn't rain? I'm not going to prepare for that!"

If he had not prepared, he would have missed out on that opportunity. What if the woman needing oil that I mentioned in the previous chapter had walked away from Elisha and said, "How will getting all these vessels help me?" She would have never seen the miracle take place in her life.

How about David grabbing five stones? David did not prepare. He over prepared. He was ready and when the opportunity presented itself, he did not miss it. If you do not prepare for things that will happen in your life, you will go through every single day the same way. You will not grow or change. You will not be prepared for the things that you want and desire. You will go through life and miss out on the opportunities that are presented to you.

Let's be honest with each other. I know in my own life, I have missed millions of dollars of opportunities in the last ten years. Not because God didn't

Billionaires prepare for life. The rest of us react to life.

want me to have them, but because I was not prepared for them. I tried to react to things that happened, not being prepared for them. A great deal presented itself. While I was trying to get the financing, getting things in order, the wealthy were buying these things up. I kept saying, "Well, it must not have been God because it didn't work out." No. It did not work out because I was not prepared! How is it not God to make $100,000?

Billionaires prepare for life. The rest of us react to life. A problem comes across a billionaire's desk and he is ready and prepared for it. The rest of us are reacting to it.

Billionaires use a portion of time each day to prepare for whatever comes their way tomorrow. If we are to become billionaires, we have to begin to prepare.

In my one-year journey, this was the biggest life changer. What is amazing is this preparation didn't take any time away from doing the other things I enjoyed doing. I found that billionaires eliminate time-wasting activities and replace them with preparation.

We waste an hour every day listening to mindless music, sports talk, Howard Stern, etc. Billionaires take that time and listen to books, CDs, anything that gives them wisdom for life. Who cares that you know all the stats for every baseball player in the league? That does not make your life any better. Take that time and that space in your mind and learn how to invest, learn stocks, learn business, learn those things that will produce in your life.

What you want in life will not just drop in your lap. Windows of opportunity will open and, if you are not prepared for them, they will pass you by. As little as twenty minutes a day spent preparing will do wonders. But you can do more. You can never over prepare. The amount of preparation that you do will determine your harvest. If you take just twenty minutes a day to learn and improve yourself, you will be in the upper 5%. You will be doing more preparation than 95% of the people in the world. You will be part of the elite who prepare for opportunities. If you take an hour a day, you will be even more rare. You can never spend too much time changing and growing and you need to continually renew your mind in the areas in which you want to be successful.

When you look at the great people in the world, you realize that they spend their whole lives in preparation. Zig Ziglar reads a book a day. And I am not talking about magazines. Zig does not read trashy romance novels.

He reads books on leadership, growth and wisdom. He reads books for understanding his life, his marriage and his children. He did not just haphazardly raise a family. He is an intelligent person who realized that he needed to gain understanding of how to raise kids and how to have a successful marriage. He used the same principles to be a leader in sales, which made room for his talents as a speaker. You have to seek wisdom and prepare for the opportunities you want. You have to be ready for the opportunities.

This book began as a teaching in church. In preparation to teach, I pulled together seven thousand pages of notes. For a weekly teaching of one hour, it takes me about fifteen hours of preparation. I am always planning and investing time on teachings. I have to be prepared so that when I am traveling around the country to talk about my book, I am ready. I have to prepare so that any time I need to teach on a Sunday morning, I am ready. I am always preparing so that I am ready for the next opportunity.

I will prepare and some day my chance will come.
-Abraham Lincoln

What are you preparing for in your life? Are you prepared? How much time did you spend last week getting ready for the next opportunity that will come along in your life? The average person does not read a motivational or teaching book in a year. How many books have you read this year? When was the last time you bought a book, read it, took notes and studied it? Our society expects to be spoon fed from television and media instead of stepping into a bookstore or library to learn and gain the understanding needed for the next opportunity.

One evening in 1955, there was a young psychologist lying in her bed. Suddenly there was a crash and a Cadillac plowed right into the room. She wasn't hurt, but the occurrence revolutionized her thinking forever. From that moment on, she knew she wanted and would have a Cadillac of her own. But she was not sure how to make that happen.

She sat in her living room (much safer than the bedroom) and watched the game show *The 64,000 Dollar Question*. Suddenly she knew how to get her Cadillac. She did not want the money. She had a goal and that was to get her Cadillac.

But while watching the show, she discovered that all the contestants had unusual knowledge about a subject that did not fit them. There was a Marine who knew everything about the ballet and there was a shoemaker who was a gourmet chef. She knew nothing about a subject that did not fit into her lifestyle.

She knew she was a young, pretty psychologist but she needed to stand out in order to make it on the show. So she chose to learn about boxing. She spent every extra minute learning as much as possible about boxing. She learned every statistic there was on boxing. She knew who was the champion in every weight class for every year for the last fifty years. She knew every statistic for every boxer who was top ranked for the last fifty years. She became an expert on boxing.

So she decided to put in her application to *The 64,000 Dollar Question* show, and she was chosen to be a contestant. Once on the show, she kept winning week after week until she won her Cadillac. But she did not stop there. Once she owned the Cadillac, she went ahead and answered the 64,000 dollar question and with the publicity she received, she was given her own show. Her name was Dr. Joyce Brothers and that is how she got to where she is today. Her level of preparation changed along with her thinking and that catapulted her to the next level. By preparing for the opportunity, she was able to take advantage of it when it came.

> **What separates you from financial increase in your life is a lack of knowledge and understanding.**

You need to know that there is a window coming and God is going to open it up in your life. Be prepared and be ready. It is going to take wisdom and knowledge in your life to capitalize on the opportunities that are in front of you. I believe that what separates you from financial increase in your life is lack of knowledge and understanding. You are where you are today because of the knowledge you obtained yesterday and all that is keeping you from increase is wisdom and knowledge.

I know two people who are in the same line of work but because of a difference in their wisdom and knowledge, their pay scale is drastically different. They are painters. One of them earns an hourly rate between $12 and $13.

The other one makes $200 an hour. They are both very good at what they do and they are both busy all of the time. Why the difference in pay?

The first one can come to your house and paint your wall any color you want. The one who makes $200 an hour can take your tan wall and make it look like marble. Knowledge of a different technique separates their skill level and their income. Knowledge and wisdom will catapult you in your business or whatever you do.

My dad was making $9 an hour in the early eighties. He wanted to earn more but you had to be a part of the union. Union workers were making $50 an hour. To be part of the union, you had to go through a special college and train.

But my dad was determined. He stopped by the union office every single day on his way home and asked if he could take the test to join the union. And every day they told him he had to go to the school and train first.

I can remember him studying an hour a night, just hoping to get a crack at that test. I would ask him, "What are you doing?"

He would say, "Studying for a test."

"When is the test?" I would ask.

"Don't know," he would respond.

"If you don't know, why are you wasting your time?"

He then said something that has stuck with me my whole life. "I'm getting ready for when God opens the door for me. If I don't get ready today, I won't be ready tomorrow."

My dad studied diagrams and everything else he could on air conditioning and heating units. Finally one day, he stopped in at the union office. The receptionist that my dad had talked to for over two years said, "Hold on." She made a call and a man came out and said, "Come back tomorrow at 3:00 and we will let you take the test."

If he had not prepared for that moment and the opportunity, there would have been no way he would have been able to study all the material in just one night. But he was prepared. He scored 95% and joined the union and started making six times as much money. He invested a little bit of time into preparing for that moment and he was ready.

Who does not have twenty minutes a day that they can spare to learn? Instead of reading the paper, you can read a book that will give you the knowledge and wisdom you need for the next opportunity that is coming your way. Learn about real estate or investing in the stock market. Prepare. It will catapult you into peace, joy and happiness in your life. Nothing can compare to gaining wisdom and understanding. Those two things will get you all that your heart desires.

Happy is the man who finds wisdom,
And the man who gains understanding;
For her proceeds are better than the profits
of silver,
And her gain than fine gold.
She is more precious than rubies,

And all the things you may desire cannot
compare with her.
Length of days is in her right hand,
In her left hand riches and honor.
Her ways are ways of pleasantness,
And all her paths are peace.
She is a tree of life to those who take hold
of her,
And happy are all who retain her.
                    (Proverbs 3:13-18)

On your commitment page, write down how much preparation you are committing yourself to. I encourage you to give at least twenty minutes a day.

Be sure to visit LifeWithScot.com for bonus video
teachings that are designed to accompany this chapter.

7

BILLIONAIRES KNOW WHAT THEY WANT
WE SEEM TO BE DOUBLE-MINDED

I *want to know all Gods thoughts; all the rest are just details.*

-Albert Einstein

There is a term used by the Harvard Business School — "cognitive dissonance." Cognitive refers to the mind and dissonance means discordant. It usually is used to describe sounds that don't belong together so they clash. In biblical terms, cognitive dissonance means double-minded. The Bible is very clear about what double-minded people can expect — nothing.

For let not that man suppose that he will receive anything from the Lord; he is a doubleminded man, unstable in all his ways.

(James 1:7-8)

When it comes to money, double-minded means that on the outside, you say you want wealth but on the inside, you believe you cannot have it. Outside you set goals and have a vision but on the inside, you do not believe you can achieve it. James says that you are unstable in everything you do. It affects every part of your life. It will affect relationships. You might be a man married to a wonderful woman but your core values cause you to believe that women do not have any worth. You don't see men and women as equal so you treat your wife like garbage. Then you wonder why the marriage has problems.

You want to be blessed in your finances, but deep down, your core beliefs hold you back. You are double-minded and unstable. You can't hold on to money even when you have it. You really believe that prosperity is not possible for you. You have to stop being double-minded.

Billionaires know what they believe. The rest of us think we know what we believe. Billionaires allow their inside thoughts to bring success into their lives. The rest of us allow our outside circumstances to hold us back from the success we should have in our lives.

Let me explain. There are two types of thinking—thinking about what is external, the things happening around you, and thinking that is internal, focused on your actual beliefs. The type of thinking that you allow to dominate you will determine your level of success.

External thinking says that there are no prosperity opportunities right now. The economy is down. The government is slowing things down. Even income is down. External thinking finds excuses for why you can't possibly prosper right now. External thinking only looks at the circumstances.

This is where we live. Billionaires, on the inside, say, "What a great time to buy up land. What a great time to start a business. What a great time to step into success."

Jesus taught Peter a lesson about not looking at the circumstances but instead, looking to what the Word of God says. I touched on this story earlier, but let's revisit it.

Peter had been fishing all night, but Jesus told him to try one more time.

> *When He had stopped speaking, He said to Simon, "Launch out into the deep and let down your nets for a catch."*
> *But Simon answered and said to Him, "Master, we have toiled all night and caught nothing; nevertheless at Your word I will let down the net."*
> *And when they had done this, they caught a great number of fish, and their net was breaking. So they signaled to their partners in the other boat to come and help them. And they came and filled both the boats, so that they began to sink.*
> *(Luke 5:4-7)*

On the outside, Peter said there were no fish. But Jesus said there were. Jesus didn't create the fish. They were already in the lake. Peter just hadn't convinced any of them to get into the fishing net. But Peter had the perception that there were no fish anywhere in the lake. Jesus had to get him to think differently. He told Peter to try it again. Peter's perception of things had to change. Peter had to think differently. When he did, the circumstances changed completely. Suddenly there were more fish in the net than he could handle.

What you perceive will eventually become real- ity. When you perceive that you can't succeed, you won't succeed. You won't even try. You are beaten before you start. If Peter had gone with his first perception, he would have quit for the day. The perception of "no fish" would have become his reality. If Jesus had not spoken to Peter, his perception would have had him quit trying right there. He would have stayed discouraged and that would have been the end of it.

We cannot allow our perception of circumstances to form our reality. We must let the reality of the Word of God inside of us form our perceptions. The way you see the world, how you identify with people, is filtered through your mind. So what you are seeing is not true real- ity. It is your perception of reality.

Let's say something happens to you today. You have to filter that event through your prior experiences, through hurts and pain that you've had in the past, and your mind dictates how you will respond. You will act according to the perception in your mind. If the perception isn't right, your reaction won't be right. And you probably won't even realize that your thinking is wrong. You'll just wonder why the whole thing didn't work out better.

Let me give you an example. One day a guy walks over to a woman at work and tells her that her hair looks re- ally nice. He isn't hitting on her. He just wanted to be nice and thought she would appreciate the compliment.

But for the woman, those words went through the filter of her mind. Her father sexually abused her. For her entire life, men have had only one thing for her. Out of her hurts, pains and her past, her mind forms the perception that he was hitting on her. Even though she doesn't know this guy or anything about him, her perception of him is already formed and she automatically thinks, "I know what he wants. He's just a pig." So she says something rude to him and walks away.

> **The way you see the world, how you identify with people, is filtered through your mind.**

Because of her perception, she may have missed out on a great friendship or possibly more. An opportunity is lost because the perception that was built up inside her didn't allow her to respond in the right way.

This is just one example of how wrong perceptions can affect our lives. When it comes to finances, it is usually even more important that we change our perceptions. We have to make sure that we look at what God says, not what the circumstances, filtered through our past experiences, tell us.

We have to stop being double-minded where we say we want to invest, we want success, but our outside thinking keeps telling us to play it safe. Keep waiting. A perfect deal will come along.

Most of us miss great opportunities because of this type of thinking. We miss the fish because we can't see past our own past. All we see is failure and this causes us to just play it safe. Like Peter, we have to be able to hear the voice of God when He tells us to drop our nets a little further out.

The investments are there for you. You can find the good things you want in life and you can prosper. But you have to be ready for them. You have to do something different than you've done it in the past. It's an old saying that the definition of insanity is continuing to do the same thing over and over while expecting a different result. You will do what you think, so if you want to do something different, you have to think differently.

You have a core belief inside of you that guides you in your beliefs, core values that were formed in you when you were young and they are shaping your future and your destiny. If those values are wrong, they create a resistant force to your prosperity that needs to be dealt with.

On the outside you may say that you really want to be wealthy and prosperous but deep down at the core of who you are, your perceptions are telling you that there is no way you could ever have wealth because it is evil. If you want to be spiritual, you have to be poor.

I've heard so many ridiculous ideas about money from supposedly spiritual people that I can't begin to tell you all of them. I've had people tell me that they knew someone who came into a lot of money and then stopped coming to church, so money must be evil. I know a lot of poor people who don't attend church, too. And a lot of rich people who do attend. The money isn't the issue. It is the core beliefs that they have.

This is just one example of the kind of religious thinking that most of us learned in church early in our lives.

It is not the way God thinks. It is just religious nonsense. God doesn't have a problem with money. You do. He wants you to be wealthy. If you do not change those core beliefs and perceptions, you will continue to struggle with money. Many people listen to the prosperity message in church and it doesn't seem to affect their finances. They are still poor because, even though they are around wealth, they still see nothing but failure in their own lives. They can't get past their core values. They think poor so they are poor. Your mind will do whatever it takes to prove itself right according to your core beliefs. You have to change those beliefs so that your thinking will allow the blessings of God to come into your life.

As it is, your core values are getting you to do things that cost you money. You make bad investments and make bad decisions that hold you down because your mind believes that you should be poor and it sabotages everything you do. It might be that your core perceptions is that wealth is a sin. It might be that you believe you are not worthy of wealth or success.

> **Your mind will do whatever it takes to prove itself right according to your core beliefs.**

Your core belief might be that you don't have the talent or ability to become wealthy. Whatever it is, it needs to change until your perceptions of yourself and the world around you are the same as God's. Whatever level you see yourself at is where you'll be.

If you see yourself as dumb, then you need to see

that the Bible says you have the mind of Christ. You might see yourself as a three or four on a scale of one to ten. God sees you as a nine or ten, but the homing device in your head locks onto the signal being transmitted in your heart and you keep going back to the three. And that's where you stay. You have to look honestly at where you are and change what is inside so that you can get to where you want to be in the future.

Implement the principles in the Word of God and start working on your core beliefs. Set goals and change your thinking to achieve them. Constantly refresh and update your heart to strengthen the right core beliefs and you will overcome every resistant force inside of you. Every day I am able to step out further and tap into God's strength. Every step I take removes more of the fears inside of me and gives me the attitude to keep moving toward my goals. The more I change my thinking, the more I give God an opportunity to bless my life.

Write down on your commitment page that you are committed to changing your core beliefs. You will see yourself able to do all things. You will stop looking at circumstances and look to God. You will not allow your past to dictate your future.

Be sure to visit LifeWithScot.com for bonus video teachings that are designed to accompany this chapter.

8
CORE BELIEFS

Change can either challenge or threaten us.
Your beliefs pave your way to success or block you.
-*Marsha Sinetar*

I love the stories my dad tells me. Occasionally he points at something and tells me that he actually invented it. He invented snowboarding. In the fifties, he and his buddies got a piece of wood and sanded it down. Then they took it to the hills. They called it snow surfing. I think that if my dad had acted on that idea at the time, when God gave it to him, our family would have billions and billions of dollars from that one idea.

In the early nineties, I had something that came up inside of me, right about the time that the Internet was getting popular. I was very involved in buying and selling cars. So I thought, what if I went to the dealerships and, for a little fee, I had them sign up to have pictures of their cars online where people could pull them up and print out a list instead of driving from dealer to dealer?

I actually started talking to people about putting this concept together but I was not sure if it would work or that it would ever take off. Today the AutoTrader has nearly three million cars at any given time signed up. At $75 a car, that is a lot of money. That was an idea given to me by God. But what was inside of me was not ready for something that big. I was never able to step out and put my nets into the water and reap the abundance God had for me. Of course, today, AutoTrader is out there and just keeps getting bigger.

There are ideas that God wants you to get inside of you but if He gives you a big idea and you have a little vision, then you will take the big idea and make it small. You have to have a big mind inside of you to be ready to handle it when God gives you a big idea.

The Bible does tell us that we have the mind of Christ, so it should not surprise us that we have big ideas. We're supposed to. And any idea that comes from God will be different than the way the world thinks. Isaiah tells us that God's ways are different.

"For My thoughts are not your thoughts,
Nor are your ways My ways," says the LORD.
(Isaiah 55:8)

If we have the mind of Christ, then we can have God thoughts. If we can have God thoughts, we can have His ways. But we have to change the core beliefs inside of us. We have to learn to speak the Word of God.

*C*hoose *beliefs that serve your soul - choose beliefs that serve the grander dream of who you choose to be.*

-Joy Page

When I was young, we did not have a lot of money. It was so bad I got a trash can for Christmas. My dad worked for $4 an hour and had to work one hundred hours just to make the mortgage payment and pay the bills.

Dad grew up in a line shack so the little that we had was an improvement on what his father had provided. His thinking was not prosperity. He didn't have that in his core beliefs.

If we have the mind of Christ, then we can have God thoughts.

What helped my parents change their thinking and get them to where today they are millionaires was the Word of God. My mom made a tape of all the scriptures she could find that spoke of prosperity. She recorded her own voice speaking the verses. She played it over and over, twenty-four hours a day, listening to her own voice telling her that she could obtain wealth. She could overcome all things in Christ Jesus. She used to walk around the house and even sit at the breakfast table and begin to confess scripture. And it made a difference in my parents. They stopped thinking poverty and started thinking prosperity. Their thoughts came in line with God's thoughts.

When you hear those things and meditate on God's Word, your core beliefs begin to line up with the Word and your thoughts become the thoughts of God. Your ways become the ways of God. Faith comes by hearing and hearing and hearing the Word of God.

You may have tried to force financial blessings into your life and it didn't work. It is because you still don't think the way God thinks. You need to meditate on God's Word, speak it and confess it every day until it becomes so ingrained inside of you that prosperity and good things just happen to you on the outside.

As your core values change, you will change. Wherever you go, you will be blessed and everyone around you will be blessed. When a company hires you, that company becomes more valuable. Everything you do becomes blessed because your mind and your core values line up with the Word of God.

And as you become lined up with the Word of God, you will find yourself acting on those ideas that God puts in your mind. So many people go through life with Jesus speaking to them but they don't take action. They tell themselves that it will never happen for them. The things that they learned from their parents, the wrong ways of thinking, keep impacting them. What is inside of them keeps them from blessing. They miss the voice of God and the idea goes by without ever becoming reality, until they see it being done by someone else.

You have to provide the right environment for a God idea to take root and become a great idea in your life. Ideas that are contrary to your core belief system will not be accepted or acted on. Unless you change your core beliefs, you will not be able to see the miracle power of God work in your life.

*A*nyone who doesn't believe in miracles is not a realist.

-David Ben-Gurion

There are two types of miracles in the world. The first type is the miracle that happens to you. My mom was diagnosed with rheumatoid arthritis. The doctor told her that within six months of the diagnosis, she would be in a wheelchair. We laid hands on her, prayed, confessed health over her and God restored her body. She is incredibly healthy today and she has never been in a wheelchair. When she was healed, the doctor said it was a miracle. That is a miracle that happened to her.

When I was younger, I was hit in the eye with a baseball. The doctor told me that I was going to lose my eye. But we prayed and God healed my eye. It is fine today and my vision is great. That was a miracle that happened to me.

The second miracle is the one that happens for you. These are miracles that you have to participate in. When Jesus told Peter to lower his nets, He could just as easily have said, "Hey, Simon, you want fish? Let Me take care of that for you." Jesus could have commanded the fish to jump in the boat. The boat would have filled up with fish and that would have been an amazing story.

But Jesus decided to perform the second, more powerful miracle, the participation miracle. The disciples had to actually go out and do something. Jesus did that to change their lives rather than just change the moment. He wanted to change what was inside of them. Give a man a fish and you feed him for a day, but teach him how to fish and you feed him for a lifetime.

The greatest miracles that will happen in your life will be the ones that require you to change on the inside and then do something. But when that miracle comes, you will be changed for life.

In the early eighties, my father was laid off from his job. Seven months went by with no word from his employer. He had us to take care of, the mortgage to pay and all the other responsibilities of life. It would have been very simple for God to do a miracle for my dad and just drop money on the porch each morning like the manna for the Israelites. My brother Jason and I could have run outside all excited, grabbing money while our neighbors fought us for it. It would have been amazing.

But that would not have helped my dad grow so that he could do bigger miracles in his life. God used the opportunity to get him to participate in the miracle. And my dad changed and grew. He leaned on the Word and read the Bible even when things did not make any sense. God said, "Don't worry about it." Dad thought he wanted to worry about it but God reminded him that He would supply everything he needed.

My dad began to put his hands to things so that God could prosper him. He bought and sold cars. He took jobs wallpapering and doing windows for people. And even though he worked fewer hours that year, he made almost $20,000 more than the prior year. God not only provided for him, He prospered him. My dad learned that God would bless the works of his hands.

Why did God do that miracle in my father's life? So that when he was set up to fail because of the circumstances, he was ready to overcome anyway. My dad worked at a local church. They sent him out to Apache Junction, Arizona, a place where everyone expected him to fail. He didn't know what he was doing. He had a congregation of twenty-eight people in a building that looked like a light wind could knock it over. But God told Dad to lean on Him and they would see it through. Dad was ready because of the miracles that had happened ten years earlier. He knew he was ready to handle bigger miracles in his life, so he put his hand to building the church and it started to grow. The first miracle catapulted him into the second miracle. God accomplished both miracles through my dad's participation.

> **God used the opportunity to get him to participate in the miracle.**

Then God told my dad that He wanted him to build a building. Dad thought, "Well, I can't build that building. That is too much money. It would take over $2 million. We can't make that kind of a mortgage payment."

But God said, "Build it." My dad was obedient so he put his hand to the task and did what he knew how to do, expecting God to do the rest. He went to the bank to get a loan and the bank said no. Everyone around him said that he could not get the money. But he knew that he and God could get it done.

The city told Dad that he could not build the building but he kept on, knowing that he and God could get it done. He spent time during the week hammering and sweeping and drywalling and then he preached on Sunday. He did everything that he could possibly do and suddenly, we were in the building and no one could believe what had happened.

God walked side by side with my dad in those first two miracles and those prepared him for the third, which is the building that we are in now, the church with three domes in Mesa, Arizona.

And God is not done yet. God said that we need a bigger building yet. That is how it works in our lives. If my dad had not been ready for the first miracle, he would never have arrived at where he is today. He is one of the most blessed people in America and he uses his blessings to bless thousands and thousands of others.

We have the most amazing opportunities ready for us but we have to step out and create the right environment so that God can do miracles in our lives. We begin to step out and do things that do not seem to make sense to us but as we participate in the process, God does the miracle and it prepares us for even bigger miracles in the future. We grow and change inside and then the change shows up on the outside. Your business grows from ten employees to one hundred employees quicker than you could ever imagine, because you are ready for the window of opportunity when it opens.

Life is all about windows of opportunity. Many people miss them because they simply are not ready for them.

They haven't filled themselves with the teaching they need and they talk themselves right out of success. They have not created the right environment to allow God to work in their lives.

Jesus couldn't do many miracles when He went to Nazareth. Why? Because of the environment created by the unbelief of the residents. Even Jesus had to have the right environment to do miracles. The unbelief of the people caused them to miss the opportunity that was there.

Often when people hear about the things that happened to my dad, they want to feel sorry for him. They think it's so sad that he had to go through so much. But James shows us that the problems we overcome make us stronger, facilitate change and teach us patience so that we lack nothing.

My brethren, count it all joy when you fall into various trials, knowing that the testing of your faith produces patience. But let patience have its perfect work, that you may be perfect and complete, lacking nothing.
(James 1:2-4)

Every time we experience a setback or something happens to us, we need to see it as a window of opportunity that can bring a miracle into our lives. When God speaks, you need to listen and act on what He tells you. Otherwise you will miss that opportunity.

A person's preconditioned thinking will always determine the material level that they reach in life. Your heart governs your purchase patterns, what you will invest in and how you do things. You make many decisions every day and 95% of them you make without giving it a thought. You are on automatic pilot most of the time. You just react to things. When you are driving your car, you don't think about things like hitting the brake or the gas. You just do them.

Unfortunately for most people, they react to great opportunities the same way they do with everything else. They miss them because what is inside of them is not ready to participate in the miracle or the investment. So the opportunity goes by as they sit back and wait for God to do something else. To succeed, you have to trust God but trusting Him means participating in what He is doing. It means training yourself and being ready. It means stepping out and taking a risk.

In the commitment part of the workbook, write down that you will be committed to participating in the next miracle God puts in front of you.

Be sure to visit LifeWithScot.com for bonus video teachings that are designed to accompany this chapter.

9
YOU ALREADY FAILED
IF YOU DON'T TAKE RISKS

*H*e who is not courageous enough to take risks
will accomplish nothing in life.
                                        -Muhammad Ali

Ask any billionaire how he got where he is today and he
will say, "Risks!" You cannot achieve success without stepping out. We stay average because we play it safe.
Billionaires became wealthy because they stepped out and
took a chance. We say, "What if we fail?" Billionaires say,
"You fail if you don't take a risk."

Every billionaire has failed thousands of more times
than you and me. Most billionaires have gone bankrupt
at least one time, some multiple times. Most billionaires
have had more than three businesses go under. They have
lost millions of dollars in business ventures. Yet they are
billionaires today.

We, on the other hand, have never been bankrupt.
We have never lost a business. We have definitely never
lost a million dollars. Yet we struggle each month to just
pay the bills. What is the difference? RISKS!

*D*o you want to know who you are? Don't ask.
Act! Action will delineate and define you.
                                    -Thomas Jefferson

In one year, I have become a millionaire. How? RISKS! I began to think like a billionaire concerning risks, and it literally changed my life. Though people all around me said, "Land is going to crash, don't buy, don't step out," I said, "If I don't take a risk, I will never get out of this financial situation." Even if land does fail, worst case, I get right back to where I am today. With this knowledge, I will gain. I know if I keep trying, there will come a point when I don't fail.

Life is full of risks. We face them every day. If you want to have any success in life, you have to be willing to try some things, take a few chances and step into areas that are new and often unfamiliar to you. Most people spend a lot of time talking, but not much time doing. The wealthy don't think that way. They are willing to actually do something.

In all labor there is profit,
But idle chatter leads only to poverty.
                                    (Proverbs 14:23)

You have to study and learn but you also have to work and apply what you learn for success to happen. If you just run your mouth and tell everybody that you do want to be wealthy and that you are going to do so many things, but you don't follow through, it is just idle chatter and it leads nowhere. You may know someone who has been talking about the same great idea for the last ten to twenty years and they are convinced how much prosperity it will bring, but they continue to do the same things in life day after day. You catch up to them twenty years later and they have not changed one bit.

> **In life, everything we do that has a reward to it also involves some risk. There is no reward without risk.**

*H*e who risks and fails can be forgiven. He who never risks and never fails is a failure in his whole being.

-Paul Tillich

One of the principles that you have to commit to is becoming a person of action. In life, everything we do that has a reward to it also involves some risk. There is no reward without risk.

You cannot go from crawling to walking without the risk of falling down. When a baby decides that he does not want to crawl for the rest of his life, he will keep getting up and falling down until he learns how to walk. He would not be rewarded with walking or running if he did not take that risk.

If you want to date, you have to risk rejection and ask somebody out first. It may take six or seven times before someone says yes, but you will have your reward when they do. I had my heart broken many times before I met Holly. I took risks so that one day I could get the reward.

You have to take risks to reap rewards. My oldest son Laken learned how to use a skateboard. At first he didn't do anything risky. He just sat on it and rolled along. Finally, he experimented with standing up. He was going down the hill, doing different things, when the skateboard flew out from under him and he skinned his elbow up. It hurt pretty bad.

The next time out, he was sitting down on the skateboard, thinking he was cool, until his friends came over and they started doing tricks. Seeing his friends do amazing things while he was trying to be impressive on his booty, kicking one leg up, was not working for Laken. He fell hard, but he wanted to have the reward of doing the things his friends were doing. So he got up and tried again. He has fallen several times since then but he dusts himself off and keeps trying, which is what we need to do, too.

God wants you to get up and take some risks so He can help you. His Word says that He will guide your steps but He cannot guide your steps if you are sitting on your behind. Step out and move a little and God can direct you and guide you into some business deals and investments that will gain great rewards.

You may make a mistake and not hear God's voice but it is just like falling off the skateboard. You have to pick yourself up. Failing at something does not make you a failure unless you stop trying. You need to step out again and again, trusting God, who is your partner, until you succeed.

The average businessman has to fail nine times before he gets that million-dollar business. But I promise you, the tenth one is worth all prior failures.

If you take no risks, you will suffer no defeats.
But if you take no risks, you win no victories.
                                        -Richard M. Nixon

I believe life is like the game Monopoly. How well do you do when you play Monopoly? Are you content just going around the board and collecting your $200 because buying the properties is just too risky? Do you win the game if you play like that? No, the person who is buying Boardwalk and putting buildings up all over is the one who wins — just like in life. You cannot continue to go back and forth to work, pass go and collect your $200, and ever hope to gain prosperity. You have to step out and take some risks. Take a few chances and before you know it, you start winning at the game of life. You have to step out and do things.

The Word of God is not passive. It requires action. You are not to be just a hearer of the Word but also a doer. Throughout the Bible, there are stories of people who took risks and got the reward. David is a great example. He had to fight Goliath, which was a huge risk, but he was rewarded when he won. Abraham had to leave his family and everything familiar to him, but he was rewarded for his actions.

How would you do if God asked you to do that to-day? What if God told you, "Pick it all up because I am giving you a new land and I'm going to make you the father of many nations. I am going to do a lot of great things for you, but you have to leave your home and family and travel to an area you have never heard of."

Most of us would tell God, "This is not comfortable and I'm not sure if I can do it now because this is not a good time. Can we wait until I have enough money in the bank?" We would not be able to step out and be rewarded like Abraham. He became the wealthiest person in the area.

After the exodus from Egypt, the Israelites were brought to the border of the Promised Land but they were held back by one thing. They were not willing to take the risk. The giants were too big. The fortresses were too strong. God got them away from Egypt, which was the strongest nation at that time. He sent the plagues and crushed the Egyptians. He showed Israel great miracles. But they still thought the risks were too great and they would not step out. An entire generation missed out on the Promised Land. Today, many Christians miss out on their promises, too, because they are unwilling to take risks. Success requires action.

What is interesting in the story of the Israelites is that without risks, God will still provide, but He provides just enough. The Israelites got just enough manna to live on. They couldn't even store it up because it spoiled.

God could have dropped abundance in their laps, but that isn't how God operates. He blesses those who step out. He blessed the next generation that stepped out and said, "Let's take Jericho. Let's get into the land of more than enough."

I believe that this is the picture for most of us. We live in the land of "just enough." No matter what we do, we can't seem to save, can't seem to get "more than enough." It isn't until you decide to take the Promised Land that God enters into the "too much" mode. I challenge you, take the land. If not for you, then for your next generation. If that first generation had taken the Promised Land, their children wouldn't have had to. They would have been brought up in it. As soon as you take the Promised Land, you make it that much easier for every generation that follows.

But someone will say, "You have faith, and I have works." Show me your faith without your works, and I will show you my faith by my works.
(James 2:18)

Many Christians want to sit back and pray, "God, where are my finances? God, bless me." They are looking for God to send money down from heaven. They run to the mailbox in hopes that God placed something in there. They continue to pray for prosperity and look up to the skies for their glory clouds. Praying for God's blessings, tithing, and working with

> **God will bless whatever you put your hands to but He cannot bless something unless you put your hands to something.**

God at your side bring you favor. The Bible says that God will bless whatever you put your hands to but He cannot bless something unless you put your hands to something.

God gets 10% of your income. You pay your bills and then you have 10% you need to mark for investments. You cannot spend that money on Coca Cola and smokes because God cannot bless those things. He is not going to make your cigarette the most amazing cigarette. But if you take that 10% and plant it in the ground, invest it, then God will bless it.

My dad taught on the power in numbers. He was talking about doubling your money every week and he used the example of a garage sale. If you start with $5 and double what you make every week, at the end of thirty-six weeks, you will have a million dollars. That is one big garage sale but it demonstrates the power in numbers. When you step out and invest, the numbers begin to go up and God has an opportunity to bless and prosper what you are working toward.

You hear a teaching or a sermon that encourages you to enter the blessings of God. Finally you decide you are sick of renting so you are ready to step out and buy a house. You are so excited and feel good about taking a chance, but then you walk out of the room and start to question your decision. "That's a little risky. What if I buy it and I can't make a payment?"

That is living your life where you never employ God. God has no job in your life because you will not allow Him to work. I want to live on the edge. I am out there where it is just me and God and I need God. I need Him to help my deals to go through and to assure that everything runs smoothly in my investments and my life.

God wants to be a part of the lives of those who lean on Him, look to Him and trust Him. He does not want to be a part of someone's life who does not have a place for Him. He has no job to perform because you do not want to step out and buy a house, but imagine if you did. In two or three years, you could have $100,000 in equity that you could use as seed to plant in your finances. If you had bought a house three years ago, you would have the seed to plant now and see the reward of taking that risk.

I had a six-month period where I talked to five people who go to groups that teach financial prosperity, and out of those five, I believe four of them were broke. Most of the teaching and the reading that is available to you has no application if it is just faith without works.

I wish everyone reading this book could get the persistence that my two-year-old, Peyton, has. I was driving along one day with him buckled into his car seat in the back and I decided I wanted lemonade. I stopped at Sonic and got one of the super tanker, seventy-gallon lemonades and then we continued driving.

I had my lemonade with me and Peyton was in back all buckled up in his harness so he was safe and secure and he said, "Daddy! Da Da lemonade?"

I thought, *Okay, I love you. Sure.* I couldn't really get the lemonade to him while I was driving, but when we got to a stop sign, I gave it a try. I reached back and through some amazing flexibility, I was able give him a drink.

He tried to take several small drinks and then I took the cup back to the front with me so I could drive.

I took another drink and Peyton said, "Da Da lemonade? Da Da lemonade?"

I said, "No, no, son," but he persisted. I told him maybe when we got home but then he started crying and I told him if he did not stop crying he would not get any lemonade. He was mad and upset in the back and crying.

Before going home, though, I had to pull in to get gas. I got out and while I was waiting for the tank to fill, I looked through the window and watched my little Houdini do his amazing work. He somehow got all the way out of his harness and started drinking down the lemonade. I started to get back in the car and he slipped to the back like I had not seen him and we buckled up and went home while I was laughing.

Too many times we just sit there and cry to God because we want something. We really need to free ourselves of the things that we have allowed to harness us and restrict us and go get the things that God has for us. We have to be people who step out and take action.

I had someone come up to me and tell me, "Scot, when you talk about your financial blessings and all of the things that are happening in your life, it makes some of us unhappy. It is depressing to us that we are not at that level."

When you are learning and getting the Word in your life, you start seeing things change. But if you get upset because someone you know is having a little better success or they are just a level above you, then the problem is your vision. You do not have a vision for change. You are not willing to step out and take the risks necessary. You won't leave what you are familiar with. So you get angry with those who have.

Getting excited about something can bring a temporary change, but it does not mean that change has occurred inside of you. Neither does it mean that it will continue in your life. Getting excited is nice but if it doesn't produce action, it is useless. You have not chosen to be a person of action or a doer of the Word.

> **If you are upset about your current reality, all that means is you are not planning on changing.**

If you are upset about your current reality, all that means is you are not planning on changing. Let me say that again. If you are upset about your current reality, all that means is that you're planning on staying there.

Let me give you an example. I had a cell phone, the nice little flip phone type. But after a year, the top would flop over. I would be on the phone trying to hold it all together using two hands and it was irritating to even try to use it. I hated it. I kept fighting with it and cursed it every day, letting it know just how stupid I thought it was. It made me so angry.

Finally on a Friday, I made a decision to take action. I decided that on Monday, I would get a new phone. From that moment on, that phone did not upset me. I laughed at it, knowing it would be replaced in just a couple of days. Even though my circumstances with the phone were the same on Saturday as they were on Thursday, I knew change was coming. The circumstances no longer bothered me.

You will know that real change is taking place inside of you, that your heart is actually changing, because you will no longer be bothered by the problems. Your determination to take action will change everything. When I know that something is going to change in my life, I do not allow the circumstances to bother me. I do not have a million dollars but my heart has changed. I know something better is going to happen.

Although my circumstances have not changed, I am excited about life. I get excited when this person is blessed and that person is blessed because I know that I, too, will be blessed. When I had my old, stupid phone I would get upset and want to know why other people could have nice phones while I was stuck with that stupid one. But once I anticipated the coming change, I was okay.

You have to do the things that will make you successful and happy. You have to begin to believe you will receive success and happiness. You cannot just sit where you are. You have to take some risks or you will never move beyond where you are right now.

Buying land is an area of stepping out. Some of you will do it next year and others will be ready in a couple of years, but you need to buy land as soon as you can. I believe the greatest investment right now is land. I am sure people around you have said, "Oh my, I remember when I could have bought an acre of land for $20,000." Now you hear people saying, "I could have bought that land for $50,000!" When does there come a point where we say, "If I buy land today, in a couple of years it will be worth…"

Determine now that you are going to be one of those people who can say, "I bought land several years ago for $400,000 and today it is worth a million."

I know that three years ago, you could find lots for $150,000 an acre in the area where I have been looking to build a house. Now that same land is $500,000. Had I known what I know today, I would have purchased the land and made $350,000 on that one piece of property. It hit me as I was putting this all together, "Why don't I step out today? If I'm going to teach this, I should do this."

> **Life is a river and God wants us to drink it up.**

I had to do some research and figure out what I needed to do and I said, "Okay, I can do this!" Land that was $150,000 three years ago is now worth $500,000. That is a profit of $350,000, which would be about 50% interest on the bank's money. If I take a loan from the bank and pay them 5% or 6% and make 50% myself, that is amazing.

That November, I bought a lot for $215,000. In January, I sold the same lot for $275,000. In two months, I made $60,000. Pretty good, huh? That is twice the annual income of an average person here in Arizona and I made it in two months. Thank you, God, that whatever I touch is blessed.

But the thing you need to see is that I had to take a chance and step out. I had to do some things and put some things in order. I had to go and arrange the loan. I had to look for the property. I had to sign the papers and commit myself to the purchase. I had to make sure that my credit score was high enough. I had to take some risks.

It's great to make sixty grand on a land deal but you can make more if you build houses on the land. I am employing God because I need His help building a house. It will cost me $580,000 to build 4,600 square feet of house. When it is done, I will have an investment of right at $1 million.

I am building it for $110 to $120 a square foot. But the house has already appraised for $350 a square foot. It is not even done yet but it is already valued at $350 a square foot. In a worst case scenario, I can sell the house for the $350 per square foot and make $1,610,000, which is a profit of $610,000. Not bad, folks! Am I a builder? Am I the one out there with a hammer putting this together? No, but I am the one stepping out and taking a risk.

All of this is available to you. I'm not doing anything that you can't do yourself. Life is a river and God wants us to drink it up. He wants us to be prosperous but He needs you to step out. Take some risks and give God a chance to prove Himself to you. Get committed with some other people. Start forming partnerships and begin to investigate and share how you are going to make it happen. If there are six of you and you make a profit of $610,000, everyone will receive $100,000 on one investment.

I am not doing anything special or different than anyone who has accumulated a million dollars has done before. Look into the lives of the millionaires out there. The

money did not just fall into their laps. They took a risk.
But if they could do it, I can do it. And if I can do it, you
can do it.

In the workbook on the commitment page, write out
that you will become a risk taker. You are getting out of the
wilderness and you are taking the Promised Land.

*If you're not making mistakes, you're not taking risks,
and that means you're not going anywhere. The key is
to make mistakes faster than the competition, so you have
more chances to learn and win.*

-John W. Holt, Jr.

**Be sure to visit LifeWithScot.com for bonus video
teachings that are designed to accompany this chapter.**

10
YOU ARE A MAGNET

You are a living magnet, drawing to yourself the people, the resources, and the ideas you need to fulfill what you expect. To the successful it is out of their faith, for others it is out of their fears. If you don't like what you attract, don't change what is coming towards you, change the magnet that is bringing those things into your life
                                        -Scot Thomas Anderson

You will attract the people, the ideas, and the resources that go with your most dominant thoughts and expectations. Basically, whatever you really believe, your subconscious will work at bringing you the tools you need to produce it. You are a living magnet. You attract the people, the ideas, and the resources you need to accomplish the expectations you have set within you. Your expectations are bringing your life to you, just like a magnet. Whatever is in your subconscious mind, the most dominant thoughts, the expectations that you have, your mind will attract.

Your mind will attract the people you need, the finances you need, the ideas you need, to fulfill your expectations. If you expect a bad day, your mind will bring everything you need to fulfill that order. You expect a bad night with your spouse; serve it up hot, because here comes your order. If you change that and expect a great day, you get what you ordered. If you are full of fear about what the future holds, the future holds what you are afraid of. Fears are negative expectations. Your fears are attracting everything you need to produce what you fear in your life. In the next chapter, we will discuss how to get over those fears, but for now, I want you to be aware. They are producing. You need to get rid of every fear you have.

If you fear your business will go under, it will. But if you have a sense of confidence inside of you, you begin to attract the people and the ideas you need. This does not mean that your business is guaranteed to work, but it means that in the course of time, it seems like all of a sudden, you will have attracted the resources and the ideas you needed to catapult one of your businesses into success. It may be your first. It might be your seventh. But that confidence will bring success.

Your mind attracts what it needs to fulfill what is expected. What are you attracting in your life? What is the one thing you can change that will change what you attract? Your expectations!

Be sure to visit LifeWithScot.com for bonus video teachings that are designed to accompany this chapter.

11
THE CORRIDOR PRINCIPLE

*F*ootball is like life - it requires perseverance,
*self-denial, hard work, sacrifice, dedication
and respect for authority.*

-Vince Lombardi

Dr. Ronstadt, a professor of entrepreneurship did a study of the entrepreneurs going through the business program of a college. For twelve years, he studied these young adults, trying to find the reason why some went out and had a great deal of success (became very wealthy), while others did not see that level of success, but instead, just got a job and blended in with society.

He found that there was a difference between those who were successful and made a lot of money and those who did not, and it had nothing to do with their grades in school, nothing to do with their I.Q., nothing to do with their race or color, their past, their parents, or their upbringing. The only difference he found was that the ones who were successful had the courage to launch businesses with no guarantee of success.

Dr. Ronstadt came up with what he called "the corridor principle." He said:

"When you launch towards a goal, no matter the distance, you begin to move down a corridor of time. As you move, doors of opportunity will open that you would have never been able to see unless you had stepped out!"

That one insight will change your life! As you begin to step out in life, with no guarantee of success, doors of opportunity begin to open up for you that you would have never seen had you not stepped out.

This is exactly how the wealthy do it. This is exactly why we aren't wealthy. We sit around waiting for the opportunities to come to us, for wealth to drop in our laps. You have been waiting fifteen years for the planets to all come into alignment so you could start your business. You've been waiting for the money, the people and the resources to drop in your lap. It never has happened and never will happen. But once you step out, the law of attraction attaches to your faith, which then brings the people, the resources and ideas you need to accomplish it. But you never would have gotten these things had you not stepped out.

This is the way I conduct my life right now. When a door opens, I will go through it. When a business presents itself, I will do it! But the doors are down the hallway. YOU CANNOT SEE THE DOORS OF OPPORTUNITY UNTIL YOU STEP OUT! The doors will not come to you. You have to step towards them. It is time to get moving.

When you do, you will see doors of opportunity that you never knew were there. The interesting thing is that they were always there. They were just up a little way, just a couple steps beyond what you could see.

You say, "You know, when I have money, I will invest." No, no, no. To get lots of money, you will have to invest!

"When I have some security, I will take a risk." But that's not a risk then. "If I have a guaranteed business, then I'll do that." No, no, no. That's not a risk! Without risk, there is no reward in your life. You have to step out in your life and then you will get.

Do you see how this works with expectation? I step out because I expect. If I didn't expect, I would not step out. My stepping out is in faith of what I expect. This activates the law of attraction, which then brings to me everything I need for success. You cannot see the doors of opportunity until you step out!

What happened in my life was that I stepped out, and as I stepped down that corridor, my minds suddenly began to attract whatever I needed to have success. All these people had been there for years, but I would never have attracted them until I stepped out!

When I finally decided that I would buy land, I didn't have the financing and I didn't have a lot of money in the bank. All I had was a realtor and good credit. I found some land and said, "I want it. Write a contract."

Two days later, a guy came into my life who got me zero down financing. A week later, a builder came across my path who could build for me for cheaper than anyone else. I found out a guy who had been my friend for years did architecture on the side and would draw up my plans for half price. I had been waiting for years to buy land, waiting for the financing, and the builder, the architect. Once I stepped out, all those doors became available to me.

One of my really good friends, just five years ago, was broke. I remember helping him move from his apartment, thinking, *Let's just burn all this junk rather than wasting time moving it.* I thought of giving him $10 for all of it, just so we didn't have to move it.

Over the past five years, he has put into practice the principles in this book. His first business had instant success for six months, but then the industry changed, and it tanked. I asked him what he was going to do.

He said, "I'm starting a magazine."

I said, "What do you know about that?"

He said, "Not much."

I said, "Who will write the articles?"

He said, "So far, just you—I hope."

I said, "Who will print it?"

He said, "Don't know."

"Do you have advertisers?"

He said, "Not yet. But in thirty days, we will have our first issue. I need my article from you by Friday."

He was laying it all on the line, every penny he had. He was stepping out into something that had no guarantee of success. He stepped out and, boom, Robert Kiyosaki and his wife, the number one finance best-seller of this decade, wrote an article. Then John Maxwell signed up to do a monthly article. He got Miss America. He got two Phoenix Suns players and a PGA player to contribute an article. All this was in the first two months. His magazine instantly had enough advertisers. In three months he is making, after paying all the bills, $40,000 plus a month.

All of that was right there all along, but he couldn't see it until he stepped out.

I wonder what is down your corridor. What million dollar ideas, companies, books, sales—what doors are waiting for you? You will never know until you step out!

Let me give you an example in my own life. My father-in-law, a few years ago, brought an amazing toy home from China. It was shaped like a pig head, soft plastic, with water inside. When you threw it at the ground, it splat out flat and then slowly came back to shape. It was amazing.

Right away, I began talking about how there is nothing in the United states like this toy. Now the old Scot would have talked about it, how cool it would be if I could get them. And of course do nothing with it. But the new Scot believes in stepping out.

I did some research on the Internet and found nothing. Finally I asked my father-in-law to talk to his interpreter see if he could find out anything. We finally got a photo of the packaging, it was in Chinese. I paid a guy to interpret it and then call the manufacturer on my behalf. Well, the manufacturer basically said they would not sell to us. Old Scot would have given up, new Scot knows better. I asked the interpreter to go to the company and see what he could work out. Well, the interpreter said the same thing, he couldn't find anyone who would sell to us. I asked my father-in-law how much his interpreter made. He said he made about $100 a month. I told the interpreter I would give him $300 if he found a company that would sell to me. Wouldn't you believe it, a miracle happened. The next day, he found a company for me.

The company would not sell to me, even talk to me, unless I ordered 50,000 of these toys. What in the world was I going to do with 50,000 splats? I had no one to sell them for me, no store connections, I had nothing. But I believed in the corridor. I believe if I step out, God will bring to me the people, resources and ideas I need to sell the toys. Plus I figured if I couldn't sell them, I had Christmas presents for the rest of my life.

I ordered the 50,000 splats. At that time, I had no idea how we would even get them from China to me. A few days later, a broker and shipper just happen to show up in my life. Once I got the splats in my garage, I met a few people who wanted to sell them at swap meets. In less than thirty days, I had five companies ordering from me. I then learned about these toy fairs. We started going to these things. In just six months, we had 50 companies ordering from us. In our second year, we landed in all the Knotts' Berry Farm parks, and Cedar Amusement Parks along with Ripley's Believe It or Not. This last year, we handled the public school fundraising company. Next year, they will order a half a million on their own.

Do you see how stepping out brings everything you need into your life? Had I waited until I had people to ship the splats, and waited for companies to want to sell them, I never would have had this success. The door was too far down the corridor.

Be sure to visit LifeWithScot.com for bonus video teachings that are designed to accompany this chapter.

12
TRY, TRY, TRY, TRY - OH, AND TRY AGAIN

If I had my life to live over I'd like to make more mistakes next time. I'd relax. I would limber up. I would be sillier than I have been this trip. I would take fewer things seriously. I would take more chances. I would climb more mountains and swim more rivers. I would eat more ice cream and less beans. I would perhaps have more actual troubles, but I'd have fewer imaginary ones. You see, I'm one of those people who live sensibly and sanely hour after hour, day after day. Oh, I've had my moments, and if I had to do it over again, I'd have more of them. In fact, I'd try to have nothing else. Just moments, one after another, instead of living so many years ahead of each day. I've been one of those persons who never goes anywhere without a thermometer, a hot water bottle, a raincoat, and a parachute. If I had to do it again, I would travel lighter than I have. If I had my life to live over, I would start barefoot earlier in the spring and stay that way later in the fall. I would go to more dances. I would ride more merry-go- rounds, I would pick more daisies.

—Nadine Stair

If you try something enough times, you will succeed. If I hit enough golf balls, I will get a hole in one. It might take ten shots. It will probably actually take a few hundred thousand, but if I try enough times at something, I will succeed.

> *Do the one thing you think you cannot do. Fail at it. Try again. Do better the second time. The only people who never stumble are those who never mount the high wire. This is your moment. Own it."*
> *—Oprah Winfrey*

How do we use this law in our favor? Well, if you start enough businesses, you will have a successful one. It may take three. It could take seven. Maybe ten. But if you try enough times, under the law of probability, you will succeed.

We hear that nine out of ten businesses fail, and we say, "I'm not going to try that. Those are some horrible odds."

A successful person says, "Do you mean I only have to start ten businesses to get a successful one? Those are some great odds." Once again, who cares that the first nine flopped? In the end, I win. With Business Ten, I made a million dollars.

Colonel Sanders retired at sixty-five. All he had was a fried chicken recipe that everyone said he should go into business with. He came up with a plan. He would give his recipe to a restaurant at no risk to them. All he wanted was a cut of the profits.

He went to his first restaurant. They said no. He went to a second. He went to his twenty-fifth. How many of us would have stopped at two? Maybe one? He went to his one hundredth. How many stop there? How about 500? How about 750? What about 1,000? I don't think I know a single person who would not quit after 1,000 rejections. That is a lot of outcomes (or failures, depending on your attitude).

On try number 1,007, Colonel Sanders got a yes, and the rest is history. He used the law of probability. If I ask enough people, I know I will get a yes.

E<small>*ver tried? Ever failed? No matter, try again,*</small>
fail again, fail better.
—Samuel Beckett

This is my story of two friends. The names have been changed to protect the ugly. My two closest friends right out of high school, we will call Tim and Chuck.

Tim was one of the most handsome men you will come across—6'2", strong jaw, with that rugged manly look about him. If you asked any woman about him, she would say, "He is hot."

Chuck, on the other hand (I will try to be nice about this), was pretty ugly. It looked like God was rushed, and He didn't have enough pieces to finish poor old Chuck. He looked like a big old weasel that was shoved onto a corndog stick.

Chuck and I were not too close in high school, yet I was amazed at how many hot girlfriends weasel boy got. Poor old Tim was just trying to scrape together a date for prom. You will see that natural talent does not mean success. Risks mean success.

As a good Christian boy, this will trouble my mother to read. We had this dance place by Arizona State University (Home of the Sundevils) called "The Devil House." It's just a dance place where I thought I could go and meet the Proverbs 31 woman that God had for me. Of course, I could never tell Momma I was going to the Devil House, so I had to tell her we were going to a Christian Campus Bible Study. "Tonight, Mom, was awesome. We really dove into the book of Corinthians." (Sorry, Mom. It was done for the greater good.) The Devil House was wall-to-wall gorgeous women, and I was sure God would want me to go after the desires of my heart. It was truly the Promised Land flowing with silicone and honeys. (That is funny, but sorry, Mom, for writing that.)

Out of high school, Tim and I were best friends, so for the first four months, we went to Devil House together. Tim, the handsome one, and I would go in, pay our money, and walk right by all the gorgeous women, making sure not to make eye contact. We would then walk right over to the pool tables and play pool for the rest of the night.

As the gorgeous girls walked by, we would talk about how next time, we would ask them to dance. They passed by again, "Oh shoot, I missed her again. Next time I will ask her to dance." At the end of the night, we would be driving home, talking about all the girls we almost asked to dance. We talked about how next time we would get a dance. We did this nearly every weekend, most of the time

Friday and Saturday nights, and then Sunday night for high school girl night.

Needless to say, I became an amazing pool player. Then one day Chuck and I started to hang out. One night Chuck said, "Let's go to the Devil House."

I said, "Sure." I loved to play pool.

Remember, Chuck is no Tim in the looks category. So we paid our money. I was headed for the pool tables when all of a sudden, in front of me, Chuck walked right up to two gorgeous girls, both of whom were a foot taller than me, and asked them to dance. I almost wet my pants! Fear shot through my body. I started to tremble. They looked at us like we were dirty little pieces of trash found on their shoes, chuckled at us and said in the meanest tone I have ever heard, "NO!"

I wanted to cry right there. I needed some counseling right that moment, because I had been emotionally wiped out. I grabbed Chuck and said, "What are you doing? We are supposed to play..."

Just then, he grabbed two other gorgeous girls and said, "Would you like to dance?"

I let out a high pitched scream only dogs could hear. They said, "NO!"

In my sternest voice, I said, "Chuck, knock it off or I am going to kick your..."

"Hey, ladies, would you like to dance?" They said, "No!" I wanted to just crawl into the fetal position and suck my thumb. "Please, Jesus, come now," I begged. "I want the rapture. I'm out of here. I cannot take this pain."

Just then, I heard two girls say, "YES."

I said, "What?!"

"Yes, we would like to dance with you." All of a sudden, all those nos meant nothing. I got a little rhythm moving up my leg, a little boogie in my soul. The next thing I knew, I was dancing, yes, dancing, with two of the hottest girls I had ever seen. I praised the Lord, telling Him, "You can take me now. I have lived life to its fullest."

The dance ended. I ran off that dance floor right up to the first two girls I saw. I said, "You want to dance?"

They said, "No." I went to the next. They said, "No." The next said, "No," but with the fourth, I heard once again those magic words, "Yes."

I screamed, "I knew it. If I ask enough girls to dance, there will be one that is desperate enough to dance with me."

For the next year, I went every weekend and I danced with hundreds of gorgeous women. The law of probability was working in my life at age eighteen. It had nothing to do with talent or looks or a good upbringing. It had to do with risk.

Many of you are sitting in the pool table area of life, waiting for a hot deal to come find you. It ain't gonna happen. It is time you stepped out and said, "You want to dance? You want to dance? You want to dance?" If you try something enough times, I know you will succeed.

I learned to look past the nos. Who cares about the five or six failures? It was the one amazing, awesome dance that made all the other failures go away. Remember, if you know in the end you will get a dance, who cares about all the people who turn you down?

Every millionaire, every billionaire failed at businesses before they found the business that made them a million. You have to get it in your mind that if you try enough, you will be successful.

System of Success (S.O.S.) Exercise

This is Scot Anderson's Dice Game of Probability. For this exercise, you will need two dice. There are over two million millionaires in America today. Over one million of those millionaires started out with less than one thousand dollars. One million of the self-made millionaires failed more than ten times in businesses. When they did finally start the right business, the average rate of their return was a hundred times. That's average. Some people made fifty times their investment. Some people made 200 times. Some made 500 times. The average rate of their return was 100.

What I want you to do is pick a number between 2 and 12. Write that below beside the word "business." Every turn, you will pick a number. You will do a little math here to keep track. Every number you pick represents a business that you start. You will start off with a thousand dollars. I don't care who you are. If you put your mind to it, you can come up with a thousand dollars to start a business.

In the investment column, write how much you are going to invest. I have to let you know that there is a huge chance you will fail. The odds are greatly against you. You can, if you want, just hold onto your $1,000 and not risk losing it. What you are going to do is roll both dice. If you do not roll your business, as you probably won't, you lose that $1,000. Each roll represents three months, so every three months, you can get a new $1,000. If you happen to hit on your business, you get 100 times the amount you invested. Now, go to the next line and write in your new investment. Once again, you risk as much as you have. If you have zero, don't forget to get your new $1,000. But if you have $10,000, you can risk it all or part of it. See how long it takes you to become a millionaire.

Business (your #):
Amount Invested:
Number You Rolled:
Made or Lost:
Your New Total:

Here is an example of one of my rounds in this game. It is not my best. In fact, it is closer to my worst. Realize that I have never not become a millionaire in this game. First of all, I picked the number 7. Why? Seven has the best odds of coming up. Just like in business, you can start any business you want, but there are better businesses to start than others. There are businesses with better odds. Starting your own restaurant, you have a nine out of ten chance of failure. If you start a franchise restaurant, you have only a five out of ten chance of failure. The odds are better.

Forget that garbage about starting a business you love. Those business fail more than any others. You know what I love? Making money. Start a business that makes money. Once you have lots of money, start a business you love. I risked all $1,000. It's like starting perhaps an eBay business, something cheap, inexpensive, with little start up cost. My first roll is a 6. I lost my money.

For the next three months, I reinvest another $1,000. Once again, I rolled a 6. I did this eight turns in a row. I rolled a number of 9s, a number of 4s. Do I quit, give up? I have invested all I have for three years. "Let's just stop. This will never work."

No risk, no reward. Finally, nine rolls and $9,000 later, a 7 comes up. That was nearly 3 years. But I hit $100,000. I am going to now risk $10,000. I don't think it is wise to put all my eggs in one basket. So my next business venture might be writing a book. This might cost around $10,000. Maybe I will buy some property with $10,000 down. This time it only took three rolls to hit a 7. I am now a millionaire.

Now let's invest $100,000. Let's start that dream restaurant. Six rolls later, I now have $10,000,000. It took me less than five years. It took some big risks. It took me sticking in there for nearly three years, failure after failure. Do you see how the principles work with the law of probability? The whole purpose of that exercise is for you to be able to picture the process. You start a business and in ninety days, it's not working? Either tweak it or scratch it and start another. It still didn't work? Do another. Finally, your business hits. Now do something bigger.

Be sure to visit LifeWithScot.com for bonus video teachings that are designed to accompany this chapter.

13
BEAT THE ODDS WHEN IT COMES TO
STARTING A BUSINESS

In the stock market, everyone is trying to beat the odds. Go to Vegas, it is about beating the odds. Why don't we ever hear about trying to beat the odds in starting a business? Of course, there is always a chance we will fail, but why should I just play the game to accept the odds given? Why not play to win, do things to put the odds in my favor? So nine out of ten business fail? How do we improve our odds so that if it does fail we minimize our loss? How do we improve our odds so the business is a success? That is what this chapter is about.

God says be faithful in the little and you will become ruler over much. This one scripture is what this chapter is about. Most business fail because they were started too big, too fast. Business is like math, I can't go in and take calculus if I haven't taken algebra. I can't take algebra until I know addition/subtraction/multiplication. There is a growth process, a learning process.

If I want to run a marathon, I don't go out tomorrow and try and run twenty-four miles. I would fail. I go out tomorrow and run a mile, maybe two. Next week I may shoot for three miles. The reason most businesses fail is business people try and do calculus when they haven't even learned how to add and subtract in the business world. They start off too big. They saved up $50,000, they take another $50,000 loan and go out and start a restaurant because they have Auntie's secret recipe. Two years later they are shutting down, having lost it all. Now I don't mind the failure, because we can learn a lot. But I would rather have failed losing a few thousand dollars and learned the same lesson.

In the next few pages, I will open your eyes to how to better the odds and lessen the risk. I will also deal with those people who have a great idea, yet never start a business. Usually this occurs for the same reason, they don't know the benefits of starting out small. I think we have all heard the phrase "Don't despise small beginnings." When we get done with this chapter, not only will we not despise small beginnings, we will be excited for them.

All of this material is taken from my own experiences. I have started over fifteen businesses to date. I have had only two that lost money. My limo company lost a few thousand dollars, no big deal. With one of my first companies, I made the exact same mistake we are talking about here. I started too big, and lost big. Other than that, all of my other business have made money. Some I shut down because the time wasn't worth the money. In that phrase is some great teaching. If I have two businesses, one that has huge potential and one that has small potential, where should my time go? Of course to the one with greatest potential.

My toy company, splatback, has taken years to build, but it is huge. This year we will sell over a million toys. It is from this company we will learn.

Would you be willing to work 20 hours a week for five bucks an hour? Most people, if not all, would say no. "Come on Scot, my time is valuable." Once again, I want to talk about potential. The first two years of splatback, I made no money per hour. It was all seed that I was sowing. Today, I do very, very, well per hour. Once again we have to look at the potential of our hour.

What if I asked if you would work for $1000 an hour. Most everybody would do that all day long. What if I told you the two were the same. No wealthy person started out making $1000 an hour, they started making nothing an hour. But they saw the potential in that hour. They sowed the seed and waited patiently until one day their hard work produced a harvest.

Let me drive the point home with a great example. You have a secret chimichanga recipe that is amazing. Most families do one of two things. Most families do nothing with that recipe but talk about what a great restaurant they could start with it. Generations have been talking. But talk hasn't produced anything. There are a few families that would save up their money and start a restaurant with the $100,000 they saved and got loans for. From the example in the beginning, the restaurant failed because it was beyond their capabilities.

Before I go on, let me explain business levels. I teach that there are ten levels of business. Each level of business is the foundation the business is built on. At each level we learn important things so we can go on to the next level. The problem with most start up business is they try and start at level four. They skip three levels of learning and growing. Once again they are trying calculus integrals when they haven't learned how to do fractions.

Based on business levels, we should take our chimichangas and start at level one. This means I find a place to start selling them, while I just make them out of my house. I noticed at kids' baseball and football games there really isn't any good food sold. That is where I would start. Invest in a table, and maybe some warmers for the food. Buy that first weekend of food. My total investment is maybe $250, rather than $50,000 for a start-up restaurant.

Say I go out that weekend and I sell 20 chimichangas in eight hours. With those, I sell some drinks and chips. I make $40 profit. Some would say that was a waste of time. Okay, how much did you make that Saturday watching football? I think it was $40 less. You learned a few things from that weekend and also, some of your customers told some friends about your chimis.

The next weekend you sell 60 chimis and you make $100. Now let's say that is what you do every week (I believe it will still grow each week, but for this example, let's do worst case). Now this is important! Your profit does not go into your pocket, it goes back into the business. So for one year, you make $100 a week and at the end of the year, you have $5000 in your business account. Remember when you said you wouldn't work for $5 an hour? Even at $5 an hour, you put $5000 away you wouldn't have.

In that year you learned quite a bit about sales. You also made some connections that helped you get your food cheaper. You learned what sold and what didn't. You are now ready for level two business, so you take that $5000 and you buy two chimi carts and you get two locations. Now with the nice cart and with the additional location, you make $500 a week profit. At the end of the year, you have $25,000 in your business account.

In that year you learned more about sales, about taxes, about employees. You learned how to cut costs and raise profits. You built a decent customer base. You are now ready for level three. You take the $25,000 and you purchase five better carts and upgrade your current carts. You are now in seven locations, one of which is in the downtown area by the major ball parks. You are now making $3000 a week profit. At the end of the year, you have $150,000 in the bank.

Now we are ready to start our level four restaurant. When I do get a location, I have all my carts advertising for me so I start out with a huge customer base. I have my food connections, my employee connections, and I have people I can put in management positions. I have learned more in the last four years than any Harvard graduate. My restaurant and seven carts make me $25,000 a week, not including my salary. Finally I can quit my daytime job. At the end of the year, I have over a million dollars and am ready to take this business to level five.

Do you see how, in just five years, we went from $5 an hour to being a millionaire. There is a lady who heard my teaching and started doing shaved ice at the kids' games. In just two years, she now has three locations and three very nice shaved ice booths. She makes over $1000 a weekend after just two years.

What is your idea, your family recipe, or invention? How do you start a level one business? Start an Ebay business, a book business, a lawn business. If you start small, work hard, and learn, you greatly increase the odds that in just a few years the harvest will be rolling in.

My toy company has taught me more about business than all the books I have read put together. I learned it takes a lot of hard work, patience, and learning to make a business successful. But three years later, the harvest is huge.

"Scot, when should I start my business?" I like what Jesus said. He said you keep saying the harvest is in four months. Look up, now is the time. I say not next month, not next week, but right now. Every day you waste is another day you have to wait for the harvest. Plant today, and you speed up the time in which the harvest will come.

Start a level one business today!

Be sure to visit LifeWithScot.com for bonus video teachings that are designed to accompany this chapter.

14
BILLIONAIRES USE THE BANK'S MONEY

A life lived with integrity - even if it lacks the trappings of fame and fortune—is a shining star in whose light others may follow in the years to come.

-Denis Waitley

What is it that most of us want financially? Ask nine out of ten of us what we want financially and we will say, "To get out of debt." That seems to be our main financial goal. Our goal is to get back to zero.

Billionaires don't want to get to zero. They want to get past the billion mark. Most us are making double car payments, extra house payments, thinking that if we can get out of debt, we will be financially free.

Billionaires think so differently. If I can take the bank's money that I am paying 6% on and I can make even as low as 7% on that money, I have made 1% on their money. This doesn't include all the tax deductions I get on my house.

During the last year, I refinanced my house and took out the $100,000 of equity that I had. Yes, my payments went up $500 a month. Yes, I am in debt another $100,000. To the world, it seems I went backwards. To the wealthy, they see that I used that money to make a million dollars. I paid 6% to the bank on that money, roughly $6,000. I made a million dollars, roughly 1,000%. According to the world, I went backwards. According to the rich, I leaped forward. When I refinanced, I had many tell me it was a mistake. "Come on Scot, keep paying off that house." I just kept saying, "That isn't how the wealthy think."

I have more money than I have ever had in my life. I also have more debt. I have over $13 million dollars in loans. Of course, those loans will make me millions of dollars. Without the loans, I could never make the millions.

The wealthy realize that there is good debt and bad debt. Bad debt takes away your ability to make money. Good debt gives you the opportunity to produce money. You have to change your thinking about debt.

With that thought, I want to go into a discussion of one of your most important assets. That would be your credit. People don't realize that your credit score can be the difference between millions of dollars you make or millions of dollars you spend. I will spend the beginning part of this chapter talking about how important integrity is and how it relates to credit.

I realize that not all billionaires have integrity. Many of them have stepped all over people, stabbed people in the back, or gone back on deals. But they are the ones who need the drink, need the drugs. They have no peace in their lives. They gained the world but lost their souls.

I want you to realize that people are always more important than money. That needs to become a core belief. I will never give up a relationship for money. Because of this, I would never cheat someone or intentionally wrong someone for financial gain. Relationships to me are more valuable than money. Money is easy to attain. Great relationships are not.

You have to realize that you were created for relationships. That is in your DNA. You were created to walk in love. Jesus summed up the Bible in two commandments—love God and love others. Cover to cover, that is what the Bible is about.

> **The wealthy realize that there is good debt and bad debt.**

When you are not doing what you were created to do, you will not live life at the level the Creator intended. You will not have the joy, the peace, the fulfillment God intended you to have until you are doing what you were created to do. It is in your DNA.

In a cheetah's DNA is the need to hunt down the zebra. The cheetah feels alive running after the zebra. Now you take that cheetah and put him in the zoo and, yes, life is okay. Life is average, but it isn't the way it should be. Your life may be average, maybe okay, but I'm telling you, until you are creating and maintaining great relationships, you are just like that cheetah. Trapped! People have to be more important than money. Relationships have to be more important than money.

What good is it for you to become a billionaire but to lose your kids to drugs? You got the money, but along the way you lost your marriage. I'm telling you, doing it

God's way, you can have your cake and eat it, too. I have the money, but I also have a great marriage. I have abundance, but I also have a great relationship with my children. Why? Because relationships are a priority in my life. I'm doing what I was created to do.

With that in mind, let's talk integrity. Integrity is one of the greatest attributes that you can have in your life. It is the opposite of double-mindedness. Being double-minded means being unstable. Integrity means thinking the same way all the time, being consistent and stable.

Some time back, we decided to put a pool in our yard. It required getting a loan so I called a couple of different companies to get quotes.

One company kept dragging their feet. Summer was coming and it was getting hot and I really wanted that pool so I started to get impatient. The other company gave me a quote and I was so frustrated with the first company that I just went ahead and accepted it.

The very next day, the first company finally called me. And their quote was $3,000 less. Many people would try to figure out a way to get out of the deal, but I had given my word and I thought it was a good idea to keep it. That's integrity. As Christians, our word needs to mean something. Our yes has to be yes and our no has to be no. Damaging my integrity just wasn't worth a few thousand dollars.

God has a way of honoring our decisions, though. A few weeks later, the company I had the loan with came back and told me that they had miscalculated and they wanted to redo everything. When it was over, I had saved $4,000. If you do things the world's way, you will end up missing the best God has for you. If you do things God's way, He'll always watch your back and you'll end up better off than you ever could any other way.

Proverbs 22:1 says that integrity is more important than riches. Riches, favor and everything else will come to you if you have integrity. I have seen people get rich for a moment and in the blink of an eye, it was snatched out of their lives because they lacked character. They had no problem looking a man in the eye, shaking his hand and promising to deliver something while having no intention of following through on it. I guarantee you that if you conduct your affairs that way, you will have sorrow even if you do manage to obtain wealth or riches.

People who lack character and integrity build their lives without these principles and when the money comes, it is easy for them to go off into their worldly ways. It is then easy for them to leave their spouse, abandon their commitments, and take the easy road, thinking it will generate so much more but in the end, they come to the realization that it didn't produce anything but heartache, depression and a lot of bad things in their lives.

Your Credit Score

Showing your integrity as a Christian is having your yes be yes and your no be no. It means following through on what you say and keeping your word. It means living so that your word really is as good as gold. In business and financial terms, it means that you make payments on time and you do what you committed yourself to do. You finish jobs on time and you do good work. It means that you develop a good work ethic. You don't come in to work late. You don't leave early and you do your best while you are there.

What is your work ethic? Someone is paying you to work. Are you giving 100% or do you take long lunches, leave early and goof off? Understand that you are sowing seed. One day in your business, you will reap a harvest. Good character isn't something you do when you feel like it. It is something you live.

Starting today, you should give 110% on the job. Your goal should be to make your boss successful. If you are faithful where you are, God will find a way to raise you up. If you give excellence when excellence isn't needed, life has a way of giving you excellent opportunities. If you give average, expect average opportunities.

One way integrity shows up in your finances is in the form of your credit score. A good credit report is vital for business and investing. It is sad to me to think there are Christians out there who do not have the integrity that it takes to have a good credit report. Basically, when you are taking out a loan, you are committing to do everything in your power to make sure you pay what you owe every single month. When you sign that contract, you are pledging your word.

Your credit score reflects how well you kept your word. It will determine how much your monthly payment will be on different loans and it will determine the loans that you qualify for.

Last year, when I was trying to get millions of dollars in loans, it would have been impossible to do without a great credit score. My credit score allowed me to make millions of dollars on the bank's money.

If your credit score is bad, there are things you can do to improve it. So for the next six months, you need to work on raising your credit score above 660 at least. It will be even better for you to raise it into the 700s. In the workbook, I have listed different things that will help you raise your credit score.

I want to show how a good score can bless you in your life and how a negative score can actually steal money from you. Suppose you are going to take out a car loan of $20,000. I have different credit scores listed—great, good, average, bad and, of course, horrible. Interest rates will vary according to your credit score and for our example, we have great at 3%, good at 5%, and average at 7%. Right off the bat, you can see the difference in monthly payments.

Great credit of 700 or higher makes a difference.

Car Loan: $20,000

CREDIT	Great	Good	Average	Bad	Horrible
Interest:	3%	5%	7%	10%	27%
Payments Paid:	$360	$378	$396	$425	$610
Overall Interest:	$1,550	$2,646	$3,761	$5,500	$16,650

In the workbook, you see the difference between great and average credit is $750,000 in a lifetime. That seems like a lot to me. The difference between great and bad credit is just $1.5 million.

The same is true when it comes to getting a home loan.

Home Loan: $250,000

CREDIT	Great	Good	Average	Bad	Horrible
Interest:	3.8%	5%	6.5%	8.5%	Unable
Payments Paid:	$1,165	$1,342	$1,580	$1,922	to get
Overall Interest:	$170,000	$233,120	$318,800	$442,000	house

In the workbook, you see the difference great credit makes. The difference between great credit and good credit is almost $4 million. The difference between great and average credit is over $10 million. The difference between great and bad credit is $18 million. And horrible credit costs you over $50 million in a lifetime. That seems like a lot. That seems like a reason to get great credit.

You can see how much a bad credit score will cost you. It is very important that you take steps to improve it. First, we'll look at some of the things that will lower your score. Then you will be able to make the changes necessary to raise it.

The very first thing you need to do is simply not be late on your payments. It is a simple principle. When you are late making a payment, it shows up on your credit record and a thirty-day late drops your score considerably.

If you have a late payment on your credit report, I encourage you to hire a credit building company to fix it for you. I pay $40 a month to a company and that is all they do. They fix your credit and help you raise your score. In six months, they have raised my score forty points. The money I have already saved in loans will pay the $40 a month for the next ten years.

The second thing you need to pay attention to is how many times and by whom your credit is pulled. I had a friend who went out looking for a new car. He went from dealership to dealership and every time he got a little interested, he gave them his social security number so they could pull a credit report. After going to twelve different dealerships—and having his credit pulled twelve different times—he saw his credit score drop forty to fifty points in one day.

You need to make sure you have found the car you want before you give someone your information so that you protect your credit score. I knew someone else looking for a home who had a company shop them out. As a result, their credit was pulled forty times which dropped their score almost eighty

Horrible credit costs you over $50 million in a lifetime.

points. You will have your score pulled, there is no way around it, but you can take steps to minimize how many times it is actually pulled.

The third thing that will adversely effect your credit score is having the balance on a credit card over half of the limit. If you have a card with a credit limit of $1,000 and you owe $600, that will pull your score down. Pay the cards down and keep them down.

The fourth thing impacting your credit is having too many installment payments. Whether for auto or student loans or interest free payments on your television or computer, they all impact your score negatively.

The fifth thing impacting your credit is having too many credit cards or not having enough. You need to have two or three major credit cards in your life and your limit should be one third of your annual income. So if you are making $60,000 a year, then you should have $20,000 in available credit. This makes your score go up when they see that you have this much available to you and it isn't too much.

If you have too much credit, they get nervous because they know you have that much available and you could go in and take it out. All you need available is one third of your income.

Having a great credit score will come in handy when I show you Scot's 0% interest credit card. Most people owe money on at least one credit card. Those who owe are paying 5%, 12%, high teens or maybe even 22% interest on that card.

Five years ago, Holly and I were paying interest on our credit cards. We owed $10,000. I wanted to get out from under that. What I did was find a way to pay interest free, which I will teach you.

You need to have two credit cards while maintaining your good credit. You can call one of the credit card companies and tell them you love them and you want to transfer all of your money to them and you want 0% interest. With your good credit, they want you to transfer.

You do that for the six-month period. Then you give the other company a call. When you reach the end of that six months, you do the same thing. Once you do it a couple of times, you can call the company you are with and ask them to extend the zero interest period. You do this once a year instead of every six months. The one thing you want to check is if they have a transfer fee. It is generally 1%. You can negotiate with the company to see if they will waive it.

If you have decent credit, you can contact your credit card company and get a lower interest rate. If you're paying 20% now and you get an offer for 6.9%, you need to take the time and help yourself save money so you can invest it. It is money that you can be using in your life.

Credit is such an important area that you need to take notice and make sure that your credit score is as good as you can make it. It is a matter of integrity.

I do not claim to be the great credit score fixer. I strongly encourage you to hire a company that will help you fix your credit. My credit is in the mid 700s but I still have a company working on it. Why? Because I don't believe you can ever have too high a credit score.

On your commitment form, be committed to three things. One, that relationships will be more valuable than money. Two, that you will live a life of integrity—your yes will be yes and your no will be no. If you say it, you will do it. Third, you will raise your credit score.

Be sure to visit LifeWithScot.com for bonus video teachings that are designed to accompany this chapter.

15
BILLIONAIRES HAVE MORE PROBLEMS
THAN YOU AND ME

*I*t's not that I'm so smart, it's just that I stay with problems longer.

-Albert Einstein

Nothing happens in life just because you want it to. You have to make some effort. There will always be obstacles to your progress, but you have to start thinking differently about the problems you face. They cannot be things that cause you to give up. They have to be overcome. They can be conquered.

Everything in life has what Tom Landry calls a resistant force. If you want to fly, you have to overcome gravity. If you want to win a football game, there is another team in your way that you have to overcome in order to score points. If you want to get ahead in certain areas of your life, there is resistance that has to be conquered. You have a vision and to reach it, you have to get past certain obstacles in your path.

A lot of people think they can just pray the resistance away and have nothing else to do with it, but it doesn't work that way. Life is filled with problems and nothing in life is really fun unless you have something to conquer. A mountain that is easy to walk up is not fun to climb. Satisfaction comes when the mountain is steep and your footing is unstable. That's when you enjoy the challenge.

When you have something big, like a business idea, you bring God into it and together you make it happen. You conquer the resistant forces and you find much joy in the success. There is great satisfaction in conquering something bigger than yourself.

The problem with obstacles is that they make things more difficult. They get in the way of your plans. My son Laken had a birthday party and before all of his friends came over, he wanted to make up some plays so that when they played basketball, he would be ready. He got it all planned out. "Okay, Dad, I'm going to run up here, turn around and then run over here, fake this way. Then you give me the ball and I'll bounce it twice."

Well, you guys remember how magical those kinds of plays were when you were nine. We imagined ourselves scoring every time, with the crowd going wild. It worked every time. We always outwitted the defender.

Of course, in real life, it isn't quite the same. Once the other kids were there, Laken tried as hard as he could, but nothing worked the way it did when we were practicing. You have to have a plan to get around the resistant force and realize that there are things that will get in your way. But when you are prepared, you can succeed and you have a chance to win the game.

When the Philadelphia Eagles prepare for the Superbowl, they practice a lot of different plays. They score every time when the defense isn't on the field. But that isn't enough to win the game. To be successful, they have to identify the resistant force, the plans of the opposing team, and determine how they will react to it. They have to figure out what they will do to score points and win. The defense won't just roll over and let them by.

This principle is true in your life. What is your resistant force? What stands between you and success? You have to identify it and figure out how you are going to conquer it and be successful in whatever you are doing. You must think differently so that you are not intimidated by the obstacles. You must think of obstacles as challenges that you can easily overcome because you have God helping you.

> **There is great satisfaction in conquering something bigger than yourself.**

Think of what obstacles might be standing in your way. I know without asking that they are only obstacles because you believe they are. Many Christians, for example, are intimidated by the devil. Ask them what the resistant force is in their lives and they will tell you it is Satan.

But according to Scripture, Satan is under your feet and he has no power over you. If you are tithing, then he can't even touch your property. According to Malachi 3, if you are a tither, then your things are protected. If you don't

ssed. force to you. Your
stuff will break down. Nothing you touch will be blessed.
Any seed you plant, any investment you make, is not going
to produce in your life and Satan will keep taking things
away from you. He will keep you from being successful if
you don't tithe.

But that's a problem that is easy to fix. Start tithing.
Once you become a tither, the devil can't touch your stuff
anymore. Everything starts to go the other way. Your seed
becomes prosperous. Whatever you put your hands to will
be blessed. Things won't break down so often. You will
keep your stuff instead of losing it.

*Within the covers of the Bible are the answers
for all the problems men face.*
-Ronald Reagan

So Satan is not the resistant force that can't be overcome. Neither is your neighbor or your boss. They aren't
keeping you from trying some new things and getting new
ideas. Your neighbor isn't stopping you from starting a new
business. Your boss isn't the one preventing you from investing. Those things are not the problem. The only thing
holding you back from success is YOU. Everything that
might ever come against you can be overcome very easily
except for your own perception of yourself.

As a man thinks, so is he. If you believe you can't
succeed, then you can't. It's just that simple. The resistant
force that needs to be changed is you and how you think.
That's where the Word of God comes in. It says in 3 John

1:2 that a man will prosper in all things just as his soul prospers. As your soul is prospering, as the inside of you starts to prosper, the rest of you will prosper, too. Your body will have no choice but to produce prosperity in your life.

*E*very problem has in it the seeds of its own solution. If you don't have any problems, you don't get any seeds.

-*Norman Vincent Peale*

It is the core values of your life that matter. What you have inside of you will come out in every part of your life. The amount of money and blessings you have is determined by what is inside of you. It is just a fact of nature that what you believe and how you think will produce everything else in your life.

> **If you believe you can't succeed, then you can't. It's just that simple.**

If you could take any wealthy person and get inside his head to see what he thinks and believes, you would find that what is on the outside is a direct reflection of what is on the inside. You would see that they are producing exactly what they believe and what they think.

You may be struggling with wrong thinking that was instilled in you as a child. If you want to become wealthy, you will have to change what is inside of you so that it lines up with God's Word. As you are on the inside, so you will be on the outside.

We work very hard to get a problem-free life. Our prayers seem to be concerned with the removal of all our problems. We believe life will be great once we have no problems. Billionaires know that problems are what make life so great. Problems are where millions are made. We ignore problems. Billionaires conquer them. We try to get away from problems. Billionaires go after problems. We want a problem-free life. Billionaires know that problems are what life is about. Until we begin to think like billionaires concerning problems, we will never reach the billionaire point in our lives.

The man who has no problems is out of the game.
-Elbert Hubbard

One day, some time back, I was working in the kitchen, doing some bills. Heath, my ten year old, was doing some homework. He came over to me and said, "Dad, I can't do this page."

Being the good father that I am, I said, "All right. I would love to help you. Give me one minute while I get out of this program."

He replied, "Thanks, Dad." Then he put down his pencil and paper next to me and took off.

"Son, where are you going?" I asked.

"Outside. Just put it in my backpack when you're done."

Obviously, if that was how we got his homework done, it wouldn't have helped him much. He wouldn't have learned anything. If he wants to get into the fifth grade, he needs to be able to solve the problems that he has in the fourth.

It got me thinking, though. I wonder how many Christians have that attitude toward God when it comes to problem solving. "Here You go, God. Fix my marriage. I don't plan to change anything to learn how to be a better husband, but You make my wife okay with that. Fix my finances. I know I haven't had a job for a couple of years but I'm really too busy right now. I do witness to my neighbors every day and I think that's really important, so if You could just lay up some wealth for me, that would be great. You just make it all better. I'll be outside playing."

Problem solving is an important part of success. Most Christians just want the problems to go away. But God tells us that we should learn from them. We are to overcome them. If you are a child of God, then you are an overcomer.

For whatever is born of God overcomes the world. And this is the victory that has overcome the world— our faith.   *(1 John 5:4)*

We have been designed to overcome the things of the world. Problem solving is a skill that you need to master. I call it a skill because it is something that you can learn and develop—and you have to if you want to be successful.

The ability to overcome is a characteristic of all successful people. They think differently about the problems they face. They tackle problems head on. The successful, that 5% group that we want to be a part of, do not avoid problems. They overcome them. Romans 12:21 says, "Do not be overcome by evil, but overcome evil with good." God would not ask us to overcome problems if it was not possible to do so. That means that we can and must overcome.

Successful people welcome challenges. They look for mountains to climb. The average person tries to find a way around mountains instead of climbing them. They try to circumvent or avoid problems. They try to get away from any negative circumstances in their lives, so they avoid and never face their problems. Of course they never grow or change either.

James tells us that we should learn to think of problems as something that will do us good.

My brethren, count it all joy when you fall into various trials. But let patience have its perfect work, that you may be perfect and complete, lacking nothing.
(James 1:2-4)

We all like the ending of this verse. "Perfect" and "lacking nothing" are things that appeal to us. But we often forget that the way to get there is through "various trials." It is the testing of your faith that produces perfection and abundance.

When you start to think like the successful, you will see problems in a different light. You will begin to attack problems in a different way. The stress and fear and anxiety that weighed you down in the past will disappear as you partner with God to solve problems in your life. If you want to move to the next level, you have to become a problem solver, not a problem avoider. How successful you become in life is based on how you handle problems.

I have seen so many Christians who think success means having God take away all of their problems so they can have a great life. Understand this. The more successful you are in life, the more problems you will have. When my dad had a church of a hundred people,

> **If you want to move to the next level, you have to become a problem solver, not a problem avoider.**

he had a few problems. Now the church is over 7,000 and he has a lot more problems. Success brings problems with it. But the more problems you solve, the better your life will be.

If you are a problem solver on your job, your boss will love you. You will become irreplaceable in his life. He is going to give you raises and promotions and do anything he can to keep you there. Do you want job security? Become a problem solver. There are plenty of problem finders in every business. Problem solvers are the ones who rise to the top because they are so rare.

In fact, I wonder sometimes if God would rather that we bring Him solutions instead of just problems. He did say to speak to the mountain and it will be removed. He didn't say talk about it or ask Him to remove it. He said,

"Speak to it." God gave us the ability to think and to reason. He is always there to help us but He expects us to participate in the solution. It is for our own good.

I recently saw a documentary on the Discovery Channel. It showed the process of how new chicks get out of the egg. The chick starts to peck at the shell, a little at a time. It takes forever but he keeps working at it and working at it. As I watched, I noticed that the mama hen just stood there and watched.

Why don't you help? I thought. *Just kick the stupid egg so we can get on with the next show. You could have that chick out in a few seconds.*

But at the end of the show, they answered my question. If the mama hen helped the chick get out of the shell, the chick would die. As the chick is pecking at that shell, it builds up its circulation. It increases its strength. It builds up endurance. It strengthens the muscles that it will need to survive once it is out of the shell. If the mom helped, the chick would die.

We live in a world today that wants to take away everybody's shell. We want to make it too easy for people. We don't want competition because we think it will harm those poor undeveloped emotions. We don't want to have a score for a basketball game because we don't want any kids to lose. We want everyone to be the same.

I will yank my child out of any program like that because he needs to learn. Life is about winning and losing. It is about competition. If you don't learn that, then you will never become a problem solver. I can teach my child more through one loss than he would learn in a lifetime of being the same as everyone else. I want him to learn the importance of perseverance, of not giving up. I want him to learn that he can face adversity and overcome it. I want him to work at his skills until he becomes the absolute best that he can be. I want him to learn that he can handle the pressure because if he is going to be successful in life, he will have to face pressure and overcome it.

If kids don't learn those things at an early age, what will happen when they are adults and working at their first job? As children, they didn't do well with time constraints and they were told that it was okay. They should work at whatever pace they are comfortable with.

Now the boss wants a project done by Thursday. What will they say? "Sorry, I'm not good with time restraints. I'll get it done sometime, but I'm not really sure when." That kind of training won't help your child in the real world. You have to teach them to handle pressure and overcome it.

Types of Problem Solvers

There are three types of people in the world. Which type you are will determine the level of success you have in your life.

The first type of person is the quitter. This person will come to a mountain or a challenge in life and just quit. He can't imagine ever getting past the problem. This is the person who will settle for a job, work forty hours a week, retire at sixty-five and live for weekends and that two weeks of vacation every year.

Quitters do not change. They go through life without ever learning anything or growing. These are the people that you have known for twenty or thirty years and they're exactly the same now as they ever were. They have the exact same problems. They still complain about the same things. They still put up with the same things that they complain about. They have not resolved or solved a problem in decades, and they never will. They have quit.

The second type of person is the camper. This is the average person living today. Campers are excited and ambitious when they get out of high school. They can hardly wait to get out of college and make their fortunes. They can hardly wait. In fact, some of them don't. "Four years of college? That's a waste." So they decide to take a year off to find themselves. Most of the time they never get back and they never complete their degree.

The camper gets married and decides that life is great right there. He finds a clearing on the mountain, usually right at the spot where the climb starts to get steep, and he sets up camp. He wants the camp to be nice so he devotes his energy to buying nice things like a big screen TV and other toys that make the place comfortable.

He has the nicest campsite around but he is also up to his eyeballs in debt. He talks a lot about climbing the mountain. He intends to start a business. He probably has even done some research to find out how, but for some reason he never actually gets around to doing it. He just doesn't want to face the problems that come with climbing the mountain. It's very comfortable right where he is. He plans things but they are always for "later."

Campers do not change or grow any more than quitters do. They do things to feel better but they don't do things to be better. They stay right where they are until they are in their fifties or sixties and they end their lives saying, "I wish I would have . . ."

The third type of person is the climber. This person does not have time to sit down. He might take a quick rest from time to time but his focus is on reaching the summit of the mountain. He sets goals for finishing college and once that goal is accomplished, he sets more goals for business and for investment. He starts his ascent and he never slows down.

Climbers stop occasionally to enjoy the moment at different levels but they don't stop long. They are driven to reach the ultimate victory and achieve a sense of fulfillment. They want to be able to say, "Look what I have done."

Climbers all know people who said they were just dreaming, that they would never make it. But they didn't listen. They faced the challenges and they persevered and every problem that they encountered, they overcame. They didn't stop until they reached the top. They were problem solvers and the mountain was not an obstacle in their minds. It was a thing to be conquered.

AQ Over IQ

The world says that to be successful, you need a high IQ, a good Intelligence Quotient. It's all about the intellect. We have tests to check IQs. We do things to try and raise IQs. But it is not really the IQ that prepares you for life. It is rather your AQ, your Adversity Quotient. How well do you deal with adversity? Can you see problems, figure them out, come up with a solution and apply it?

Successful people solve 5% more problems than unsuccessful people. Just solve 5% more problems than you are right now and you will move from average to successful. An IQ test might show that you are intelligent but it does not necessarily indicate that you can solve problems. It isn't enough just to be intelligent. You have to develop some common sense. Get a good AQ and you will be able to solve problems.

My grandfather on my mother's side was a very intelligent man. He had an IQ of around 135-140. He was intelligent in an academic sense but his life had many problems that he was never able to overcome in spite of his intelligence. He was married four times. When he died, he left my grandmother in great debt. He had no real relationship with his children. He did not have success in any area of his life because he was unable to solve the simple problems that happened in his life. He could not handle stress so he retired from work at forty years old. He sat at home all day. When Grandma came home she would have to cook dinner for him while he screamed for her to come and help him with whatever he was doing. He had a high IQ but it never made him successful.

There have actually been studies done to compare the AQ, or the problem solving ability, of people who are successful and others who are not. Each was given an unsolvable problem and they were observed to see how they dealt with it.

Although they were unable to solve the problem, since it was unsolvable, those with a high AQ spent a considerable amount of effort and time trying to solve it. Those with a low AQ gave up relatively easily.

If you give any human on the planet enough time, he will be able to solve any problem.

If you give any human on the planet enough time, he will be able to solve any problem. There is no limit to what we as Christians are able to overcome here on earth. You may not think that you have a very good problem-solving ability, but the key is in gaining the confidence to know that with God's help, you can do it. Just don't quit. Face the problem, whatever it is, and figure it out. If it takes a long time, just know that the next one will go faster. The more you problem solve, the better you become. It requires persistence. Your AQ can be improved, no matter what it is. You have to believe that you can solve problems.

I was inspired by a movie I saw about a group of people who climbed a glacier that had never been climbed before. They reached the top and even though the climb was hard, they found an even greater problem in their descent because a severe storm struck them on the trip down.

Unable to see, they got lost and one of the climbers slipped down to a ledge where he broke his leg. He fell in such a way that his knee was shoved up into his thigh, causing excruciating pain.

One of the other climbers had a rope that he used to gradually help the man move down the glacier. The problem was that the rope was only 150 feet long so once they got to a certain point, the guy on the bottom had to dig in and slip the injured man down. They continued this until they came to the edge of a cliff. Because of the poor visibility in the storm, they didn't see it in time and the injured man ended up over the edge. There was no way then to get enough slack on the rope and the man knew that his only choice was to cut his friend loose or they would both die.

The injured hiker fell three hundred feet and landed at the bottom of the glacier, still alive but in terrible pain. Knowing that he would die if he just stayed there, he began to pull himself one foot at a time across the snow in the direction that he thought the base camp was. He did that for three days, often just inches at a time. He had no water. His leg was still in great pain. At a point where he felt he was about to die, he began screaming.

But those three days had brought him close enough to the base camp that his friends heard him and came to his rescue. His persistence in the face of overwhelming odds brought him to safety.

Anyone can be a problem solver. It really just means refusing to give up until you figure out a solution. That perseverance under various trials causes you to develop patience and faith. The more patient you are, the more willing you are to keep working and the less likely you are to give up. The more faith you gain, the easier it is to tap into the mind of Christ. Facing adversity head on will make you an overcomer. Just don't quit. Successful people are problem solvers.

This truth changed my life. A solution to a problem is usually just five minutes of thought away. A good solution to a problem is just five minutes away. A great solution is just five more minutes away. Many billionaires owe their success to all those times they took fifteen minutes to solve the unsolvable problem.

On your commitment form, write down that you are committed to giving fifteen minutes of thought concerning all problems in your life.

Most people spend more time and energy going around problems than in trying to solve them.
-Henry Ford

Be sure to visit LifeWithScot.com for bonus video teachings that are designed to accompany this chapter.

16

RAISING YOUR AQ

*E*very great man, every successful man, no
matter what the field of endeavor, has known
*the magic that lies in these words: every adversity
has the seed of an equivalent or greater benefit.*
                                        -W. Clement Stone

I have emphasized the fact that the wealthy think differently than those who are not wealthy. That is what
gets them to where they are. They look at things differently. They see money as a tool. They see risks
as opportunities. And they see problems as things to
conquer. They have a high Adversity Quotient, meaning that they delight in solving problems. They don't
avoid them.

   You will not get through problems by thinking, "Oh,
poor me." A victim mentality will keep you where you
have always been. You have to learn to solve problems.
You have to raise your AQ. Fortunately that is not hard to
do. But you have to be persistent and not give up on it. You
can become a problem solver.

   There are ten different things you can do to help
raise your AQ. Develop these attitudes and do these things
and no problem will ever intimidate you again.

1. Believe that God is a good God.

You have to be convinced that God is a good God all of the time. If you think that God is beating you up all the time, letting all of those bad things happen to you, then you will quickly lose your motivation to try. How can you fight God? If He's against you, then you might as well just sit down and suffer in silence.

When my children think that something bad is happening, they get very de-motivated to do anything. When they believe that I am good and that I want the best for them, that I want good things in their lives, they are motivated to conquer everything they face. It is an attitude in life that flows from their relationship with me.

The same is true with how you view God. When you realize that He does not do bad things to you, it changes your whole outlook on life. Instead of being angry with God about a problem you run into, you partner with Him to solve it.

My youngest son, Peyton, was given 4,000 ladybugs by his Aunt Kimmy. He had a bag of bugs and he just loved watching them. He would put his hand in the bag and feel them on his skin. He had one in particular that he singled out. It was his little buddy. He called it Ro Ro, after a dog we used to have named Romeo. Peyton loved to take Ro Ro around and play with his little friend. I watched them having fun. Peyton said, "Come on, Ro Ro," and they went all over the place.

But then, after a while, Peyton's tone changed. The ladybug stopped cooperating. Peyton shouted, "Come here." But the ladybug didn't move. "Ro Ro. Now!"

He kept ordering Ro Ro to come and when Ro Ro didn't come, he got mad and in a moment of passion stomped on him. Ro Ro was no more.

Too many Christians seem to think that God treats us the same way. If we get a little bit out of line He will stomp on us. They believe that He sends them sickness or He keeps them poor so that they can learn lessons and be humble.

The truth is that God wants you to prosper and be healthy. The lessons He wants you to learn are the ones that you get from participating with Him in solving the problems of life and overcoming every obstacle you run into. Get it through your head right now that God is good. Otherwise you will not even try to solve problems.

2. Believe in yourself.

The second thing you need to do if you are going to raise your AQ is believe in yourself and who you are. When you lack confidence, it binds your ability to solve problems. If you do not believe in yourself, then how can you believe in your own abilities? If you cannot believe in your own abilities, then you will give up before you have solved the problem.

> **When you lack confidence, it binds your ability to solve problems.**

It is interesting that research has shown that people usually give up on a problem right before they are presented with the solution. In counseling, I often see people give up on their marriage right before it is ready to turn around and get good. The darkest part of the night is right before the sun comes up.

You have to believe that you can do it. My dad taught me at an early age that whatever you think you can do is exactly what you will do. And whatever you think you cannot do is exactly what you will not do. If a problem presents itself to you and you believe that you will not be able to solve it, then you won't solve it. However, if you set your mind on Christ and believe that you can accomplish anything, then you will.

When it was suggested that we put a man on the moon, the majority of people said it couldn't be done. But there was a small group of men who would not accept any limitation to their thinking. It took some time, but they began looking for ways to make it happen. And it did.

If you do not have confidence to overcome inside of you, then you need to get some self-esteem books and teachings and read and listen until you have confidence in you. That is the first problem you need to overcome.

Make it an important enough issue in your life that you take some action. You would if it was something that mattered to you.

If your cable television went out, what would you do? Just sit there and ignore it? If your friends came over, would you tell them that the cable's been out for three years and you don't know what's wrong? You've prayed about it and it still doesn't work. Would you keep paying the bill every month? Of course not. You would get on the phone right away. You would not hesitate to get if fixed because that is something that is important to you.

If that is important, then how much more important is it that you get enough self-esteem in you to have the confidence to tackle problems and solve them? Lack of self-esteem will stop you from getting into the Promised Land because it will keep you from solving the problems that you will run into along the way. You have to believe in yourself. God believes in you so you should, too.

3. Look for options.

You are not alone in facing problems. Everybody has them. Successful people find solutions to problems and overcome them. They are not without problems. They just think of them differently. Everybody encounters obstacles to their destiny.

No temptation has overtaken you except such as is common to man; but God is faithful, who will not allow you to be tempted beyond what you are able, but with the temptation will also make the way of escape, that you may be able to bear it.

(1 Corinthians 10:13)

In terms of your financial success, this means that there is no problem you could ever run into that does not have a solution. You need to look for options because they are there. Step back and take a breath and it will help you find the solution.

It used to be that when I got the Christmas lights out of storage every year, I faced an insurmountable challenge. As I pulled them out of the box, there was this big ball of evil staring at me. I started tugging and pulling, which only made the tangle worse. It would drive me into a rage.

But once I calmed down and looked at the situation, I could always start finding a pattern in the mess and then, with a little at a time, I could unravel it. But I had to look for a solution. Today I've found an even better solution. I throw the lights away and buy new ones.

Stepping back and taking a breath will help you find the solution. Most people think their lives are overwhelming but that is not true. God always has a way for you. You are not going through anything that has not been experienced before. Face the problem and look for options. As your patience grows, it will get easier and easier to calm down and you will see patterns that you can work with. You will see solutions. Get focused on the solution, not stuck in the problem.

Your mind is an amazing thing. You can focus your thoughts anywhere that you want them. If you focus on something right before you go to sleep, your mind will work on the problem all night. Instead of just worrying about things as you drift off to sleep, try focusing on solutions. You will be amazed how many times you wake up with the answer. Your mind worked on it all night.

4. Do it.

If you want to have a higher AQ than IQ, then you need to do it. Most people have something happen in their lives and they come across solutions but they just won't step out and do what needs to be done. Going to college and getting your degree might be the solution. That might teach you enough to do the things in your life that will bring you success. But you have to take action.

It is amazing how many times a woman in an abusive relationship will not take action by getting herself out of that. She knows she needs to. She keeps telling herself that the guy is going to change but she never sees change except that year after year, it just keeps getting worse. The solution is to leave. Make a change.

> **There are actually only two things that will work. You either have to make more or spend less.**

It's equally amazing how often people will look at their financial problems and not do anything to fix them. They work in jobs that don't pay enough to do what they want to do in life. They're always behind on their bills. The solution should be obvious. There are actually only two things that will work. You either have to make more or spend less. At the very least, they could look for better work but most people won't take the time to do that. They just sit and suffer and complain.

Get your brain going. There are all kinds of reasons why you think you shouldn't invest. If you want to be successful, find solutions to those problems and get on with your success. Get some books and tapes and change some things. Just do it.

5. Failure is not final.

The next thing that will increase your AQ is the understanding that failure is not final. If you let your fears get to you, then you will be so afraid of failing that you will never try. However, you don't know that you will fail. The only sure thing is that if you don't try, you won't succeed. You have to take some risks.

Donald Trump would tell you that stepping out is the biggest part of succeeding in life. You may step out to start a business, realizing that nine out of ten fail, but you also know that you have a chance of succeeding. And even if you don't succeed, you know that you will learn from the experience. Failure is not the end. The gun went off and you ran to the finish line. You will start another business and you will keep at it until you are a success.

Failing is not failure if you learn from the experience and keep pursuing your dreams.

Brethren, I do not count myself to have apprehended; but one thing I do, forgetting those things which are behind and reaching forward to those things which are ahead.   (Philippians 3:13)

Learn from the past but don't let it hold you back from trying again. Keep trying until you get it right. That is the essence of problem solving.

6. Tension and fear stop creativity and faith.

The sixth key to raising your AQ is to recognize what stops creativity and faith from working to your benefit in problem solving. Most people allow the fears they have inside of them to keep them from being creative. You cannot solve a problem without being creative. You need to be able to step back and say, "If I tweak this a little" or "If I try that," let that creativity flow so that you can find solutions.

Fear or anxiety is another thing that will prevent faith from working. Fear is the opposite of faith. It will keep your faith from working. "What if something happens?" "What if I can't do it?" "What if something goes wrong?"

"What if?" is a dangerous question to ask. It comes from your fear and it will prevent you from seeking out solutions. God has a better plan.

And let the peace of God rule in your hearts, to which also you were called in one body; and be thankful.
(Colossians 3:15)

You need the peace of God to rule inside of you so that you can replace the fear that dwells there now. You have to confess the Word and call peace in. "I won't have fear. I won't have anxiety. I am going to step out into investments and release my fears and anxieties because I know that I am blessed in everything I do and I know that God will walk me through it. I will be blessed."

When you do this, your creativity will be activated. Your faith will be released. And you will become a problem solver.

7. Victims never change circumstances.

The seventh principle for raising your AQ is to know that victims don't change anything around them. Whenever you get lost in that attitude, crying, "Oh, poor me," you will stay right in the problem. You will never change it. If you ever find yourself starting to feel like a victim, you need to immediately step back and get a grip. You cannot be a conqueror and a victim at the same time. They are incompatible.

You probably know someone in your family or possibly a friend who has been stuck with the same problems for years. Looking back on that person's life, you can see that nothing has changed in the way that he thinks. If there has been any change, it was probably in the wrong direction.

You cannot be that kind of a person or you will be stuck right where you are for the rest of your life. Determine now that you will not be a victim in life. You will be the conqueror. The Bible says that you are not a victim. You are an overcomer. You will be one or the other. It will depend on your attitude.

8. See yourself as God sees you.

This is a natural step from not seeing yourself as a victim. That is not how God sees you. You need to get into the Bible and find out exactly what God does think of you. Start to get that image in your mind. When you do, it will not matter what anyone else says about you. It will not matter what circumstances you run into. You will know that God sees you as an overcomer and you will see yourself that way, too.

9. Know what you want in life.

In order to solve a problem, you have to know what you want for a result. If you don't know where you are going, it will be difficult to know when you have arrived. Make some plans. Don't waste time on things that don't contribute to your future.

> **There's no point solving a problem if you don't know why you're solving it.**

One night, Holly and I went to a movie. We stood in a fairly long line. We knew what we wanted to see before we got there, but even if we hadn't known, we would have had plenty of time to decide.

The couple in front of us didn't make a decision, however. They talked the whole time that they were standing there and then, when they got to the ticket window, they started talking about which movie to buy tickets for.

I always plan ahead so it is irritating when I have to wait for people who don't have a clue what they want to do. We all experience people like that, and it isn't limited to a movie line. To be successful, you need to set some goals so that you have a direction. There's no point solving a problem if you don't know why you're solving it.

10. Have new thoughts and knowledge.

To change a problem in life, you need to gain new knowledge and have some new thoughts about things. Your thoughts create your actions and your actions will create your results. If you want to have different results, then you are going to have to change your thinking.

Too often, we want different results but we are not willing to change any of the things that created those results. We go right on thinking the same way that we always did. Start putting new things into your mind. Read some new books. Listen to some new tapes or CDs. Change what you watch on television. Start thinking differently.

Thinking differently is really the main point of this whole book. Successful people are problem solvers. That is automatically where their minds go when they are faced with an obstacle to their dreams. They set out to fix it. They come up with solutions. They have a high AQ. You need to think the same way if you want to see your dreams and aspirations come to pass.

In your commitment section, write down that you are committed to raising your AQ.

Be sure to visit LifeWithScot.com for bonus video teachings that are designed to accompany this chapter.

17
SOME PRACTICAL KNOWLEDGE

To succeed, you will soon learn, as I did, the importance of a solid foundation in the basics of education - literacy, both verbal and numerical, and communication skills.

-Alan Greenspan

I hope that you have begun to understand that God wants to bless you and that His blessing won't come until you actually do something that He can bless. You have to prepare yourself, train yourself, be prepared and then act on the opportunities when they come along. God provides the blessing. Your part is to get ready by studying and learning how money and investments work.

I want to take the time to share a few practical things that will help improve your knowledge of some basic financial matters. Americans could save millions of dollars by paying attention to the things that they spend their money on and the process they use in doing business. By applying some common sense, you can find extra money to use as a seed for investment—in fact, you can find quite a bit of money.

One of the biggest areas that people lose money in is the purchase of cars. For years now, I have actually made money on my vehicles. I make around $8,000 a year and it really does not take much time to do it.

The first thing you need to know is that you never buy new. When you come onto the lot, the salesmen know that if they can get you in the car that smells so good and the leather feels so right, that you will buy it. But when you drive that pretty car off the lot, you instantly lose $5,000.

There is a big difference between buying from a car dealer and buying from a private party. At the dealer, you end up paying the taxes, title and registration, which bumps the cost up thousands of dollars before you even get your keys.

I am always amazed and annoyed at how salesmen work the deal when you trade a vehicle. You research and know that your car is worth $8,000 and yet they somehow tell you they book it out at $6,000. Actually, they come in lower and make you feel like they are working with you by giving you $6,000. You get $6,000 when you could have received $10,000 selling it yourself.

But you saved so much on taxes right? No. You saved $459 on taxes and instead of paying $3,541, you pay $5,329 at the car lot.

The average American gets a different car every two years which is a loss of $7 a day if you go to the dealership. That translates to two bad habits or $5 million over your lifetime.

Vehicles depreciate in value 25% the first year and 15% every year thereafter. So if you buy a $25,000 car, you will lose $6,000 the first year and by year four, you will be down $13,000. If you own that vehicle for two years, it will cost you $12.41 a day—or the equivalent of three bad habits and $9 million over your lifetime. All so you can drive a brand new vehicle.

Key Principles for Buying and Selling Cars
1. Never buy a car over four years old. It will not resell like you want it to.
2. Do not buy a car with more than 60,000 miles on it.
3. Try to buy a vehicle that still has the factory warranty.
4. Never buy from a dealer.
5. Never buy a car with a salvage title. Always run a CARFAX report. You want to avoid cars that have had accidents.

You can use the AutoTrader to find your new vehicle and use kbb.com to find out the vehicle's value. For me to consider a vehicle, it must be priced at least $1,000 below the private party value. I usually get a car priced $1,500 below value and offer $500 below that. But you need to check and see if the car has been in any accidents. Do some homework before you buy.

There are a few other things to think about that will add up if you are not paying attention. Check the tires. Also you do not want a car that is leaking fluid or makes weird noises while driving down the freeway. Be sure to ask when the brakes were last done. If you are mechanically challenged, you need to pay somebody to take a look at the car to make sure it is in good shape. A hundred-dollar-investment to a mechanic could save you thousands of dollars.

On the same day that I buy the vehicle, I put it in the AutoTrader, priced $250 below book value, and drive it until it sells. Normally, when I sell the vehicle, I make $500-$1,500. This is a great way to not lose $11,000 a year and millions over your lifetime. I spend around four hours every three to six months when I sell the vehicle and the same when I am finding a new one. And it saves me a lot of money.

Houses and Real Estate

These are the kinds of things you need to learn as you prepare yourself for wealth and success. If you don't learn them, you will not be ready when opportunities come.

The process of buying houses has made me over a half million dollars at this point in my life. This is your biggest investment and should give you a lot of capital. You can begin to buy land and do the things that I am doing with zero down. You need to have a place to live anyway, so why not have it be an asset that makes you thousands of dollars?

In the last two years, my house has made me $300,000. In Arizona, some areas are actually seeing a 35% increase annually. But even if it is only a 8%, 9% or 10% increase, it does not matter. When you take out a loan at 4% or 5% and you are making 8% on your investment, you are using the bank's money to increase yours. Plus, you get tax deductions and tax credits while you are making money living there.

There are a few things that will help you make more money when you buy a house. What I feel is the most important thing to consider when buying a house, as does Robert Kiyosaki, is to have a great realtor. A lot of people want to sell their house on their own so they can save the 6% realtor commission. You need a realtor because most of the time, they can actually get you more money than if you were to sell your house on your own. They have the ability to place it in more listings than you can, which gives you the opportunity to sell it quicker. And time is money. So make sure you get a great realtor.

This is true whether you buy an existing house or a new house. If you go to buy a new house, take a realtor with you so they can get all of the information together and they can tell you if the house will work for you. They can tell you about the neighborhood and everything else you need to know to make a good deal. Then all you need to do is put the money out there to make more. That is what a great realtor will do for you.

> **If you are over eighteen years old and do not have a house, you need to make plans to get one.**

If you are over eighteen years old and do not have a house, you need to make plans to get one. Going to college at eighteen or nineteen and getting a house is a great idea. You can have your friends move in and have them pay you rent so that it covers your mortgage payment while you are making 6%, 7% or 8% on the money. By the time you get out of school, you could have $70,000 in the bank to get you started. How cool would it be to have student loans all paid off while you live somewhere for free? Getting a house is imperative for anyone eighteen or older.

Before you go out and look for houses, you need to get your financing in order. Contact your real estate agent to find someone who can help you get pre-qualified. That way you'll know what price range you can look at for your house. If you are going to turn the property in three to five years, it is a great idea to look at a three year Adjustable Rate Mortgage (ARM). You get lower interest rates on the ARM and you are going to be buying something else in three years anyway. The savings of even 1% on your loan are huge. Make sure you do not get a mortgage with a prepayment penalty. If you have to have one, go no more than one year.

Often, people pass on the ARM because they want the security of a thirty-year fixed mortgage. But then they pay $300 to $500 more a month and sell in four years anyway. So they just wasted all of that money. You are going to sell houses and roll them every three to five years. Think of your house as more than just a place to live. It is an investment.

Once you find a house, you need to be sure to get two good-faith estimates. You need to find out what it is going to cost, the points you are going to be paying, and the interest rate of the loan. When I was buying my first house, I thought that all banks had to give you the same interest rate but that is not true. You can talk to more than one bank and don't hesitate to tell them, "You know, they are offering me 4.25% at the other place." They will usually backpedal and say something like, "Well, I can't do that well. But hold on a sec. Let me see." Which is always annoying because it seems they should offer the best rate the first time. "Well, I can do 3.9% and I will only charge you half a point rather than three quarters of a point."

If you take a little bit of time and do some of these things, it will save you thousands and thousands of dollars. Your real estate agent should be doing all of those things for you and you should ask them to help you so you begin to understand the whole process. Learn all that you can whenever you can.

In your search for a house, you need to look for incentives, especially if you are a first-time home buyer. When we bought our first house, there was an incentive for first-time home buyers and we actually got $300 a month back from the government. Our house payment was $600 a month. At the time, we were paying $600 rent for our apartment. Now we had a house payment of $600 and received $300 a month back. I dropped my monthly expenses by $300 and was gaining equity at the same time because I did some research. Go online and seek out the things available. Ask questions and get information.

There are different ways to come up with a down payment. Sweat equity will allow you to paint and do different things to work off the down payment. Or find someone who will loan you the down payment. You might look at an 80-20 loan, which allows you to take the loan over the amount the house is worth to build in the down payment.

If you have a house and are currently paying PMI (Private Mortgage Insurance) you need to deal with this issue now. I think it is the silliest, stupidest thing that was ever invented. It is mortgage insurance. The bank says that if you default on your loan, the PMI policy will pay it off and YOU have to pay this insurance. It can cost you $200 a month in your house payment and you can get rid of it when you have 80% equity in your house. Many banks will do the 80-20 loan so you can bypass the PMI and lower your monthly payment. If you have PMI right now, call to get your house appraised and get that removed as soon as possible. If you don't know if you have it, guess what? You have it.

If you are buying a house right now and it will be under $300,000, you want to buy new because the value of a house will dramatically increase in the first five years. The value of a new house goes up a whole lot more than houses that are five, six and seven years old. That is why you want to turn them over in three to five years. You can buy a brand new house and hold onto it for three to five years so when you are ready to flip it, you have gained anywhere from $30,000 to $70,000. I have seen some make $150,000.

When you go over $300,000, the houses have a lot of extras that come with them, like a good, established neighborhood, and that is why you want to look at the existing houses. When you are looking under $300,000, you want the rapid increase and the ability to move in with equity. A friend of mine named Dave was told he could move into his new house in six months. When the six months came and Dave and his family moved in, the value of the house had already increased so much that he had $100,000 in equity. He had not made one payment and he could sell the house for $100,000 profit before he ever turned the key. It depends on your price range, but when you are buying houses to make money, you need to sell within three to five years.

When you are out looking for a house, you need to pay attention to the neighborhood you are driving through. Do you have to go through a trailer park to get to the house? When you are ready to sell the house, you want to see what the potential buyer will see and how they feel when they approach the area. Nobody wants to drive through a bad neighborhood or have one really close by that is not comfortable.

> **When you are ready to sell the house, you want to see what the potential buyer sees.**

Is there a street directly behind the house? If you are backing up to a busy street or highway, it will hurt your resale value. If there is an empty lot behind or near you, it is important to find out what is going to be there. Are they going to put up a store or apartments in that big empty lot? That will hurt resale for you as well. So you need to have your realtor research the surrounding area to see what plans are in progress. You need to visit the neighborhood and even walk around at night. Get a feel for the area and make sure you do not have a bunch of gang bangers running around and causing trouble. All of those things impact resale value.

There are positive things to look for that will make your house more attractive in the future. If there is a mall coming to the area, that will increase the property's value. Nearby theaters help people get comfortable with the location and when they build a new freeway nearby that starts to attract more people, the neighborhood becomes more accessible and that adds value.

Other things to look for in the location to increase the resale potential include cul-de-sacs. A cul-de-sac is quiet and people seek them.

Backing up to a greenbelt attracts people because you have room behind you and more privacy.

Backing up to or being next to a park adds value, especially to a family looking to buy. All of these things help to resell a house quicker but they do not necessarily increase the value of the house.

Upgrades steal profit from you. For example, if your realtor checks the comps for the area and tells you the houses are going for $100 per square foot, then a 3,000 square foot house is worth $300,000. It does not matter if you put in a $100,000 pool in your backyard. The realtor is going to run comps for the neighborhood and the pool won't affect the value. Most people are tricked with this fact. As much as I love my pool, I have to admit it steals profit.

A pool will help the resale of your house but you need to know the real value it adds. If you build a $20,000 pool, it will increase the value of your house by only $6,000. So you lost $14,000 right away. It annoys me, but I will have a pool and I make sure the kids know that every time we swim it costs $100. Putting a pool in after the house is built can actually lessen what the house is worth, even though it can speed up the sale of the house.

You can buy a house for $200,000 and decide to add marble floors in the rooms, change the counter tops out and make all kinds of changes, making your investment above $300,000, but the house is still only going to sell for $220,000.

You can opt for the less expensive carpet and do your own labor, keeping your overall investment down. Tile and all the nice things may help the house sell quicker, but it does not increase the value a great deal because the comps dictate what people will offer you. You need to have your realtor run the comps in the area so you know where you are at and decide what, if any, upgrades you want to make.

Location, location, location. People always want to say, "But, Scot, I can get a bigger house if I move further out of town." This is true but let me show you the difference in a house that is in town compared to a house that is out of town.

Tale of Two Houses
Cost of Housing

	In Town	Outside of Town	Differences
Price of house:	$220,000	$200,000	$20,000
Payments:	$1,125	$1000	$125

Tale of Two Houses (cont.)
Losses from Location

Drive time: 10 minutes   60 minutes*
        *At $10 an hour the monthly difference is $368.

        You have already lost more money than you are saving on the house payment on a monthly basis.

Gas:	$20	$100	$347 monthly
Extra Maintenance			$100
		Total:	$815 monthly

It needs to be effective for you to buy out of town and to make it effective, you need the house that is located outside of town to be $180,000 less expensive. I encourage you to spend the extra $25,000 or even $50,000 more. It is more beneficial for you to be closer to work and in the area where you want to be.

Another thing you might run into is a lease option. On the surface, it might sound like a good deal but consider it carefully. Why do you think people offer lease options? Do you think they just want to help people within the community and make sure everyone gets a great deal on a place to live?

No, lease options are for people who do not have good credit so it is all about the seller. If possible, stay away from lease options because you will end up paying $300-$500 a month more than the owner is paying. They get the income and the appreciation on the house while you make the payments. If a house appreciates at 8% and the house is worth $300,000, it will cost you $24,000. Two years on a lease option will cost you $48,000 and you will not get the tax break which is around $3,000-$5,000 annually. Now, in two years, you are losing from $50,000 to $60,000 because of your credit. Get your credit where it needs to be. Buy a house in town or buy a new house and you will see that even in your first house, you will have from $50,000 to as much as $100,000 in equity and you are on your way.

Buying Houses as an Investment

The house you live in is one of the biggest investments that you will make. But the more you learn about real estate and how it works, the more you might want to invest in other houses purely for profit. Unless you get a really bad deal on the price of property, you can't really go wrong buying houses. Land has continued to increase in value for the last fifteen hundred years and it will continue to do so.

> **Land has continued to increase in value for the last fifteen hundred years.**

If you purchase a house for $150,000 and hold onto it for five years, in most cases, it will be worth at least $200,000. That is an increase of $10,000 a year. Even if you have bad credit, your payments will be around $1,000 a month. You could rent it for perhaps $800 a month.

I know what you are thinking. "That's a horrible investment that will cost you $200 every month. How can that be good?" This is another example of not thinking like the wealthy. You have to look at all the pieces.

Each year, you will put $2,400 into the house. Your renter will pay the rest of the mortgage payment, but it will cost you that much. However, the value of the house has gone up $10,000 over the same time period. That is actually a profit of $7,600, a 400% return on your money. That is not including the extra tax deductions that you will get. It is not a $200 a month loss. It is a 400% return.

If you are still renting that house in five to ten years, the rent will have increased to $1,200 a month and then you have a profit of $200 a month beyond the other increase.

In ten years, that house will be worth at least $270,000, which will give you a profit of $14,000 a year. Not too bad for a small investment. Now imagine that you have four or five houses, all doing the same thing.

You need a credit score of 660 or higher and you will have to put 5% to 10% down, so you will need a maximum of $15,000 to get started. If you do not have that, consider getting some partners. Save your seed money until you have enough. Do whatever you need to do in order to get started.

Another type of investment is what is called "flipping" houses. Someone might buy a house for $150,000 and then resell it at a higher price. It might be a fixer upper or the owner might have been behind in payments and just needed to get out quickly. Most times, they have a little equity in their house but they will lose it if it is repossessed, so they will make a great deal for the right buyer.

If you decide to invest in those kinds of deals, you can make a quick $10,000 per house. Be sure to include all expenses like your real estate costs and loan and administrative costs, but when you do it right, you will average around $10,000 profit.

You can do this with the house you live in. Buy a fixer upper, fix it up, move in and put it on the market. You can live in it until it sells. If it does not sell right away, it's no big deal because the house increases in value every month that goes by. You are using the bank's money plus you get the tax deduction. Once it sells, do the same thing again. Then you can start buying more than one at a time. In a relatively short period, you build up a tremendous amount of value in the properties that you own.

The important thing to realize is that you are no longer thinking in terms of just getting by. Your house is not just an expense that you pay every month so that you have a place to live. It is an investment that can make you very wealthy. That is how the rich think of everything they own. The more you learn to think that way, the wealthier you will become.

Be sure to visit LifeWithScot.com for bonus video teachings that are designed to accompany this chapter.

18
WOULD YOU WORK HARDER
FOR A MILLION DOLLARS?

A dictionary is the only place that "success" comes before "work." Hard work is the price we must pay for success. I think you can accomplish anything if you're willing to pay the price.

-Vince Lombardi

If I were to tell you that you could make a million dollars by working harder, would you? This is a great chapter about doing something where you are at, while God is taking you to another level. While reading this chapter, consider the life of Joseph. Joseph became one of the richest men in the world. How? He was the best at any job he was given. Whether he was a slave or a prisoner, he was the best. He is a true picture of being faithful in the little and God giving you the world.

You may see no future at all in your current job. You are right. There is no future in your job. The future is inside of you. And if you work 5% harder at your job and in life, you will see your future develop. The hard work you do at your job translates to how much money you will make and that will dictate how much seed you have to plant in investments. The faster your salary rises, the faster you will have money working for you and the faster you can stop working for the money.

The quality of the work you do is completely in your control. You can continue to do sloppy and inefficient work or you can learn to excel. That is entirely up to you.

The prophet, Daniel, stood out from everyone else because of the quality of everything he did.

Then this Daniel distinguished himself above the governors and satraps, because an excellent spirit was in him; and the king gave thought to setting him over the whole realm.   (Daniel 6:3)

Daniel was able to gain great position above all the others because he had what most Christian's lack—a spirit of excellence. Most of us are unwilling to give 5% more to our jobs. We just want to pray, "God, bless my job and I pray that You will have my boss give me a raise."

When it fails to happen, we wonder why. "I prayed. Why am I not getting any raises?"

Your boss does not have to give you a raise just because you prayed for it. And God won't force him to do it. But if you have a spirit of excellence and start working as hard as you can, doing the best that you can, taking on more tasks than just what is required of you, your boss will take notice. He will start giving you projects because he knows you will do it right and do it on time. He will get excited. He'll see you coming in early and leaving late. He'll see you take a shorter lunch than everybody else because you have the spirit of excellence in your life and he will reward that. And that is what will produce an amazing income, giving you more to invest.

I firmly believe that man's finest hour, the greatest fulfillment of all that he holds dear, is that moment when he has worked his heart out in a good cause and lies exhausted on the field of battle victorious.

-Vince Lombardi

Your boss does not have to give you a raise just because you prayed for it.

If you start to employ the spirit of excellence in your life you will be able to receive a better raise than most people. The average annual raise is 6% a year, so imagine that you work in the spirit of excellence and receive an extra 5% more a year. If you were making $21,000 for your annual salary, which is below the average salary, and get a 6% annual raise, after fifteen years, you will be making $50,000 annually. If you also get an additional 5% over the same time, you will be making $100,000. So in fifteen years you would go from an average salary with the potential to grow to $50,000 to a salary double that.

If you took that extra money and invested it, you could have thirteen to fifteen million dollars in the bank. What did you do differently? You had to work 5% harder, come in ten minutes earlier, leave ten minutes later. You had to display the spirit of excellence in your work.

God says that if you are doing anything, be sure and do it as if you were doing it unto Him. "I don't like my job." It does not matter. You need to think of it as a job that you are doing for God. If you do the job as if you were doing it directly for God, it would be a lot easier. I may not like flipping burgers as my job right now but it does not matter because I do it as if I am doing it unto Him.

Proverbs gives an interesting picture of what it means to work as though you are working for God.

Go to the ant, you sluggard!
Consider her ways and be wise
Which, having no captain,
Overseer or ruler,
Provides her supplies in the summer,
And gathers her food in the harvest.
How long will you slumber, O sluggard?
When will you rise from your sleep?
A little sleep, a little slumber,
A little folding of the hands to sleep—
So shall your poverty come on you like a prowler,
And your need like an armed man.

(Proverbs 6:6-11)

Can you work when no one is around? Do you need to have someone breathing down your neck to do your work? Do you play solitaire on the computer and act like you are working once the boss walks in the room? If the boss leaves early, can you pay attention and get your work done?

If someone has to look over you because you do not really have a spirit of excellence and will not work hard, then you are not working as if you are working for

God. You are not giving your first fruits when you are on the job and because of that, you will be stuck with 95% of society. You'll be stuck in the same mediocre job fifteen years from now, trying to figure out why this billionaire stuff is not working.

It is not working because you are not giving the extra 5%. Change it. The boss is gone and you are the only one working to get the job done. You are the one who tells everyone to stop messing around and focus on the goal. You stay late and do not submit for overtime. Those are the things the boss hears about and pays attention to and rewards.

When my dad first moved to Arizona, he followed the principle of 5% more. As he followed this principle, his life and his finances increased to a level most people will not reach in their lifetimes. When he first started working here, he would go in at 3:00 in the morning and not get home until seven in the evening because that is what he had to do to take care of his family.

In 1978, he made $4 an hour, which was not enough to raise a family, so he worked ninety-five to one hundred hours a week. Once he had mono and the doctor told him to stay home but where he worked, he had no sick time, so he cut back to seventy hours instead. That level of commitment has raised him to where he is today. Everything that he does, he does in the spirit of excellence. Whether it is giving a sermon, preaching or building a church, he has that spirit of excellence.

You need to get that same attitude of excellence inside of you. Can you work anywhere and still give that excellent effort? Can you have that spirit of excellence in your relationships, finances and everything that you do? If you do not develop that spirit, you will struggle through life like the rest of the world. You will live an average life. You will have an average job, an average marriage and go to church just an average amount of the time.

My dad was faithful in the little and he was made ruler over much. People try to start off too big in the beginning. They want to start by opening a corporation but they need to be faithful in the little first. Then God will make them ruler over much. My good friend, Derek Jordan, was faithful when he worked at Living Word Bible Church and he was so faithful with everything that God had given him. He was ready for an opportunity and left to start his own company. God said, "Okay, I can trust you with the little. You gave 100% every time with the little so now let me bless your corporation." When he started up his corporation, he had twelve employees.

Are you faithful in the little? My dad worked for a cooler company that had just a couple of employees. When he was working out in the heat, he developed a cooler kit that became popular in Arizona. Everybody started buying this kit that they could put on their house and in the span of a year, that company grew from several employees to close to fifty. My dad did not get any special reward or recognition for creating that cooler kit but he helped his company and his boss and he was blessed.

If you make someone else successful, you will become successful. Why not help your boss be successful?

Why not make your department successful? Making someone else successful is sowing a seed that will help you become successful.

Principles for Getting the Extra 5% Raise

There are some simple things that you can do to improve your life. Do

> **Getting an extra 5% raise will not be hard with this attitude.**

these things and you will be amazed at how quickly things change.

1. Identify your number one customer.

When I started working at Home Depot, they showed a video in orientation that said the customer is number one. You need to take great care of your customers but they will not be the one giving you a raise. Your boss is your number one customer and your goal should be to please him, making your boss successful and constantly asking, "What can I do to make your job easier?"

Most people go the other direction when the boss comes around. They complain about the boss saying, "He is always gone and I never see him do any work." But your attitude needs to be, "How can I make his job easier and work harder? What can I do so that he does not have to spend so much time at work?"

Getting the extra 5% raise will not be hard with this attitude and if you do not get the raise, you have still sown a seed in someone's life and God will say, "Okay, let me sow something into your life." Your boss is your number one customer so you need to figure out what you can do to make him successful. How can you bless him?

2. Make your boss successful.

If you have to work a few extra hours to complete a project, do it. Find out what your boss' goals and objectives are and help him reach them.

3. Find out what is important to your boss.

Pay attention to what your boss likes and how he wants things done. This is not always the same as the company. When I worked at Home Depot, the company said the customer was most important but the employees who spent all their time focusing on the customers were always the ones let go. You are trained to hold the customers' hands and walk them to where the bolts are, but when the manager comes in and asks why the freight did not get put away, there is a problem.

I would greet customers and tell them what aisle the bolts could be found on and throw freight all day. The boss would come in and see that all of the things that needed to get done were done and when he realized it happened while I worked, he was happy to give me a bigger raise. When I was making $5 an hour, the average raise was a quarter but I got a dollar-an-hour raise. I knew what was really important to my boss.

What is your boss continually complaining about or what needs to be done regularly? Find out and realize that when you do those things, the boss is happy and it helps you get a bigger raise.

4. Brown-nose.

When I look back on my life, I think I should have brown-nosed more. In 1991, I trained a guy named Ken at Home Depot. He became a department head within six weeks of being hired. We made fun of him because he was such a brown-noser, always asking what he could do for the boss. Within two years, he was managing a store and today he makes a six-figure salary and is worth over a million dollars. He was an amazing worker and he advanced rapidly. We would all tease him and tell him to stop, but he knew what it took to be successful and now has millions in his bank and in stock.

5. Loyalty.

Think about Joseph and how successful he was in life. He was thrown into slavery and they put him in Potiphar's house. Potiphar quickly put him in charge of all of his possessions. He must have had an amazing spirit of excellence to have been a slave and yet be trusted to handle everything.

One day, Potiphar's wife tried to seduce Joseph but he was so loyal to his boss that he said no. She got mad and because of the things she said, he was thrown in jail. But his attitude did not change. His excellent spirit helped him get promoted and he was placed in charge of everything in the jail. Because of his faithfulness, he became second in command in all of Egypt.

Joseph's spirit of excellence let him rise up among men and that is the same spirit you need to have. Joseph was loyal to all of his bosses. Never speak negatively about your boss or be around those who do because you do not want those seeds to be planted inside of you. Loyalty includes taking charge of bad thoughts. Jesus said that if you think about a woman in a lustful way, you have already committed adultery. So thinking bad thoughts about your boss is no different than saying them aloud. Every thought you have produces something in your life. Negative thoughts will produce negative fruit in your life.

6. Perceptions.

Pay attention to the perception that your boss has of you because it is generally his reality. Any time the boss saw me working at Home Depot, I was working hard. I may have been goofing off with everyone else but as soon as I saw him coming, I was hard at work.

When I was first hired at Home Depot, I started out in the lot—the worst job in the world (I thought). Your day consisted of loading concrete, drywall, sand, and when you didn't have that to do, you had to bring in those huge orange carts. All this was done out in the heat. My friend, Doug, had started working there three months earlier and let me know we had to put in our time. The quickest anyone had ever come in off the lot was four months and normally it took six months.

Understand that your boss judges your eight hours worth of work based on the few moments he sees you. My dad had taught me this early in life. I knew the managers were always in by the registers. This is where we had to haul those carts past throughout the day.

So I would walk as I got the carts, walk as I pushed them up to the door, but the second I got to the door, I began to run. After I dropped off the carts, I would run out the door, then stop and walk to get the next cart. Doug thought that was the stupidest thing ever—until three weeks later when I was moved inside.

> **Your boss judges your eight hours worth of work based on the few moments he sees you.**

I made it into the store, not due to working hard but because of the perception the managers had of me as a hard worker. I'm not saying to be lazy except when the boss is around. I am saying always work hard, but when the boss is around, work at a pace that no one could sustain.

Perception is more powerful than the truth. If your boss has a perception that you work hard, it will get you a raise. I know people who work hard and when the boss comes around, they happen to be taking a break and that is the perception the boss forms. Generally, he will see you about five minutes out of the eight hours you are there and he will form his perception of you in those five minutes. You could work really hard all day, but then the boss comes in and catches you playing that five-minute game of Solitaire. Your boss now thinks that you play Solitaire all day. Perception. Guard it, protect it, enhance it.

7. Solve problems.

Your boss does not need you to add more problems to the list he already has. He needs solutions. A boss will promote and give better raises to the people who find solutions to problems instead of bringing more to his desk. If you are not a problem solver, find out how you can become one. Spend fifteen minutes more thinking a problem through and figure out what you and your department can do to solve it. If your company or department has the same problem happen over and over, what will it take to finally solve that problem?

8. Keep the spirit of excellence raging inside of you.

Any job can get old. When I worked at Burger King and wrapped my thousandth Whopper, I was so bored. My dad told me to make a game out of it because competing with yourself will keep you motivated. My game was to see how fast I could fill an order. I wanted to be the fastest Whopper maker in the world. I loved it when everyone up front would take orders and I would be in back all by myself, trying to get all of the burgers and fries out as fast as I could. The time would race by while I worked. Get a vision that will spark that spirit of excellence at your job.

9. Be committed to excellence.

Vince Lombardi said, "The quality of a person's life is in direct proportion to their commitment to excellence, regardless of their chosen field of endeavor." An average or below average life is determined by your level of commitment to excellence in all that you do.

How do you dress? How is your speech while conversing with others? How committed are you in the relationships you have? How much have you committed to your job? What is your level of commitment to excellence? Why does anyone want to just get by and have just enough and live life spending six or seven hours a day watching television?

You need to evaluate your level of commitment to every aspect of your life. Doing the things that I listed and committing to them will produce millions of dollars in your life. What would you do for $5 million? Coming in ten minutes early and leaving ten minutes late while you work at your job as unto God will produce $5 million in your life. Is it important enough to you to change your attitude?

In the commitment section, make a commitment to work with excellence.

Be sure to visit LifeWithScot.com for bonus video teachings that are designed to accompany this chapter.

19
A Billionaire's Most Valuable Asset: The One Thing We Waste

Determine never to be idle. No person will have occasion to complain of the want of time who never loses any. It is wonderful how much may be done if we are always doing.

Thomas Jefferson

A billionaire's most valuable asset is not his money. It is not his car, his house, even his corporation. It is his time. Time is the only limited resource we have. I can get more money. I can get another car. But I can never get more time. My time here on earth is limited.

I found out that billionaires think differently concerning time than the rest of us. This difference in thinking produces millions of dollars a year. This difference in thinking is what keeps us average and pushes them to abundance.

It may sound brash, but there is a claim that I am confident enough to make. I, Scot Anderson, can tell your future. It really isn't that hard. If I follow you around for one week, I can easily be tell your future. For a week, I would take notes and watch the things you do and how you use your time. Then I would be able to tell you where you are going to be in six months, one year and even five years down the road. The Scotty Scope would be so accurate that it would freak you out.

You don't need me to do this for you, however. In the workbook is a log for you to track your activities on a daily basis and when you do this, you will be able to tell your own future. Once you actually do this, you will be able to see where your future is heading.

The amazing part of this is that you have the power to change your own future. You can look at where you are heading and say, "Wait! I'm not going toward my dreams, goals or aspirations." I guarantee, the majority of you who track your time will realize that you are not headed where you ultimately want to be. By seeing that, you will be able to make a decision which will allow you to change the future, based on the simple principle of guarding your time.

The value of time is never explained but if you watch successful people, the one thing they all have in common is that they guard their time. Time is the most valuable asset in anyone's life. Everything else is an unlimited resource. If you lose money, you can make more. If you lose your car, you can get another one. If you lose your house, you can replace it. But time is a limited resource that you can-not regain once it is lost.

Every moment that passes you by is one you can never get back. You have a certain amount of time here on earth in which you can fulfill your purpose and destiny. In that time, you can leave an inheritance and be blessed or, if you do not use your time wisely, it will be wasted and lost.

Steal my money and I will make more. Steal my car and I will get another car. Steal my clothes and I may be naked for a little bit but I will get new clothes. But if you steal my time, I will never get it back.

Unfortunately, most people do not view time this way. They do not see their time as valuable so they do not guard it. The time that they lose prevents them from setting themselves up for a future of abundance.

L et him who would enjoy a good future waste none of his present.

-Roger Babson

The billionaires realize that time is your seed. You plant seeds throughout your day based on how you use your time and in the future you will get the harvest from those seeds.

If you watch successful people, the one thing they all have in common is that they guard their time.

Where is your time going? Is it going toward your dreams, aspirations and goals or are you just wasting seed? Another six months, then another year goes by and you are still with the 95% of society who go their entire lives without ever maximizing or guarding their time and, as a result, their future never presents them with their dreams or aspirations.

But you have the chance to understand this and get it into your heart, which will allow you to change your future.

Making the change will lift you out of the majority and into the 5% of successful people in the world who got there because they guarded their time. The successful do not waste their time. They do not let it get away. They maximize every minute and every hour of every day. Time is irreplaceable in your life.

We spend all of our time trying to get things we want. Instead, if we spent our time wisely, things would begin to happen in our lives that would produce the things we want. You need to organize and structure your time. There are some basic tools that successful people use to guard their time that we are going to learn.

First, try to envision just how much time you waste in an average day. Let me give you an example of time management with marbles and two jars. The marbles are the seeds planted every day that will grow into dreams or be wasted and grow into nothing. One jar represents dreams, aspirations and goals. These are the things that we get excited about, the things we have passion for. The other jar represents wasted time. I am going to use the day of an average man. You can adjust this example to fit your own life but this is pretty typical for most people. There are twenty-four marbles that represent the twenty-four hours in a day.

Our guy gets up in the morning, takes a shower and eats, which takes an hour. That time is not really wasted but it is time not spent growing, so the marble goes into the wasted time jar. He did not learn anything new. He did not mature or set plans for success in that hour of his day.

Driving to work, he listens to Howard Stern for an hour so another marble drops into the wasted time jar. Stern made him laugh but nothing brought about change in his life or helped him become successful.

He arrives at work and for the next eight hours, he sits and just muddles through because he does not even like being there. So we drop eight marbles into the wasted jar.

He takes a lunch break in the middle of the day and talks to co-workers or daydreams about the day when he is going to be successful and wealthy, but he doesn't do anything but think about it and talk about it. And that is another marble in the wrong jar.

Driving home, he wants to unwind so he cranks up the heavy metal and bangs his head through traffic for an hour—costing him another marble.

We all need time to ourselves so our man goes to the gym. With the time he spends getting ready, working out and showering, he spends two hours and two marbles go into the wasted jar.

Our guy has a girlfriend so he has to spend an hour on the phone with her. "I love you, I love you, I love you,"—so another marble goes into the wasted jar.

A game is on so he spends three hours yelling at his team and cursing the referees. Three more marbles go to the wasted jar.

The day is almost over and our guy has yet to put a single marble in the dream jar. He would like to read a little, but he does need to get some rest to get ready for the next day. So there's really no time left. He spends six hours sleeping so the last six marbles go into the wasted jar.

And so ends a day in the life of an average man. He has done absolutely nothing to change his future. Six months or a year from now, he will be in exactly the same place that he is right now.

Your time and how you use it now is producing your tomorrow. You have to ask yourself one question. What are you producing? If you do not commit your time to learn how to get where you want to be, you will never go any- where. There are so many people who retire and wonder what happened. "I haven't experienced my dreams or de- sires but I had so many things I wanted to do when I was younger. What happened?"

What happened is that they did not guard their time, so nothing was produced. They never realized a dream or accomplished anything they wanted to do. The time just got away and they could never get it back.

*M*en talk of killing time, while time quietly kills them.

-*Dion Boucicault*

Rich people view time as their most important com- modity and it is weird to see people who are not rich judge them. Rich people get judged because they have the foresight to have others mow their lawns and clean their houses so they can use that time to go after their dreams. Time and money are directly related and wealthy people understand how maximiz- ing their time will allow them to be successful.

You can get a pretty good idea how you think about

time when you consider how you feel about washing your car. Most people say, "I'm not going to pay somebody $9.99 to wash my car. I'll wash it myself." And that is what they do.

But let's look at what it costs you to wash it yourself. By the time you get everything ready and actually wash the car, you have used an hour of your time. To save $10, you spent an hour.

But that is not all that you should think about. If you have someone else wash your car, it will take you thirty minutes to go down and wait for your car, but you could read a book while you are waiting, investing in your thought process, learning something of value. If you make use of that time effectively, it will benefit you much more than $10.

Changing your own oil is another waste of time. You can get your oil changed at Wal-Mart for $16. I know guys who spend $10 on the supplies and it takes them an hour to do a job that saves them a whopping $6. If you

What is it worth to you to devote your time to creating future success in your life?

are working on your future, that hour will be worth much more than $6.

Some of the things we do to save a couple of dollars are really time stealers and when we really look at them, they are just plain silly. At Christmas time, I had to laugh when I went to Wal-Mart. I walked in and the line for returns was just about out the front door. I understand that you need to return things but my time is so valuable to me. Unless I am returning something big, I will not wait in line.

I laughed because the guy at the end of that huge line was waiting to return a bicycle inner tube. I could not believe it. I was tempted to hand him $2 and tell him to go do something else. Surely that hour he would spend in line was worth a lot more than $1.98.

What is your potential value worth? I'm not talking about your present value, but the value of your time in the future. What is it worth to you to devote your time to creating future success in your life? If you figure out that your wasted time now is robbing you of millions in your future, you would realize that your time is worth far more than $6 or $10 an hour.

Changing your own oil will cost you $250 as will washing your car yourself. Right now you are thinking that you are not worth $250 an hour, but we are talking about your potential value. If guarding your time, measuring it and taking different steps with your time now would produce millions of dollars a year in the future, what would the value of your time be? It would be worth thousands of dollars.

All you have to do is guard your time and treat it like it is valuable. Think like the wealthy. Get past the, "I only make $10 an hour so I might as well wash my own car," kind of thinking and look at your future. You need to think, "Would I wash my car for $250?" When you begin to think this way, you get a different mind set and focus on your potential value which changes your thinking.

Here is another example of potential value. Take a bottle filled with water that is currently valued at $1. Let's say we know for a fact that in five years, the water will be worth $5,000. Would you treat that bottle differently? If you knew the potential value and somebody wanted a drink, would you give them a drink or would you guard it closely? "You want a drink of my water? Heck no!" You would put it in a safe place and protect it.

Most people have that kind of potential inside of them, but they don't recognize it and they just pour the water out. They waste valuable time that could be devoted to their future. You might share your water with someone else, but only if they bring something of value to you. Otherwise they are just stealing from your potential value.

Too many people let friends and others steal their time, robbing them of future potential. Satan knows that you will not reach your goals and aspirations if he can get you to waste your time. He will go after your time and he will send people your way who are time wasters. What we need to realize is that these people are also destiny and purpose stealers. Asking for a minute here and a minute there, they are stealing your dreams. That minute turns into an hour and when you continually stop to give them time, you are pulled further away from your destiny. Once you realize just how valuable your time is, you will begin to protect yourself from time stealers and wasters.

To be successful, you need to identify the time wasters in your life and remove them right away. This may sound cold but it is far worse for me to not fulfill the purpose and destiny God planned for me. It is wrong for me to allow people to steal all of the blessings and good things that I can do on earth just because they will not get off of their booty and work toward their own destiny. Instead they want to waste my time.

The people in my life keep the same pace I do and in order to be around me, you have to keep a quick pace. When people come into my office, they say, "Hey Scot, I have a quick question." They know that they need to ask the question and get out of my office. Those are the people who are going to be successful in life.

There are others who come in, breathe deeply and say, "Can I close the door? I need to ask you something." Then they pull up a chair. These people want to sit down and hold a long conversation, taking as much time as they can, not realizing that they are wasting their most valuable resource—time. The time they take is something that neither of us will ever get back.

I do a lot of counseling. Normally I give people some things to do before we meet a second time. If they come back and they haven't done any of the things I assigned them, I am not going to sit there and waste time with them. Most people don't follow up and when I find that out, the session is over. If you are not going to help yourself, it is not my responsibility to drag you through life and try to make you successful.

When I was in junior high, we had to run a mile every week and that was a big portion of our PE grade. We had a set time that the coach required us to finish in and when I was young, the time was easy to reach. But I found a friend who did not want to run. We would start out okay, but then he would start walking. We were friends, so I walked with him.

Nobody has the same purpose or destiny as you and your time is too valuable to continually stop for them.

We would walk and talk and have a great time but we would come in way past the time and coach would yell at us. I just brushed it off but when my report card came, my dad was very disappointed that I received a D in physical education.

I had to change and not allow my new friend to hold me back from my potential. So many have friends around who do not see the same success you do. They have different hopes, dreams and aspirations, or rather, they don't commit any time to pursuing their dreams. They waste time by sitting back and enjoying the comforts of everyday life. They walk through life when they are supposed to be running. They walk lap after lap, only to get to the end of life and find that their accomplishments earned them a D+. You may be a good friend and you are welcome to run with me, but you have to keep up the pace. I'm not slowing down for you.

In 1991, I changed my pace. I wanted to be more godly and take a full college course load. Of course, that meant that I had to change what I did with my time. I no longer could frequent the places that college kids hung out and try to meet women.

When I started changing those things, my friends did not want to participate. "Scot, come out with us." I had to say no and the result was that almost none of them wanted to run with me. It is sad, but when I look at their lives today, they still have not changed their pace in life. They jump from marriage to marriage and live unhappy lives.

If you are running with me and you fall, I will pick you up and help you get back up to speed. But if you want to sit on the sideline of life and you are trying to hold me back, I apologize, but I will not change my pace. There are so many things to accomplish in this lifetime and your time is running out. So get moving. Nobody has the same purpose or destiny as you and your time is too valuable to continually stop for them.

You have to identify your time wasters and you have to remove them. Proverbs says the companion of fools will become a fool. I cannot hang out with negative people because I get to a point where I an frustrated with them.

One night Holly and I went out with a couple and they were negative about everything. Anything we said to them, they would twist it to make it turn to the negative. I, on the other hand, can find a way to make everything positive so that entire night was exhausting for me.

When we finally made it home, I flopped on the bed. I told Holly that they wore me out. The wife was the most negative person I have ever experienced and I felt genuinely sorry for the husband. I will not hang out with negative people. They slow down my pace. If you want to run with me, you have to be happy, positive and upbeat. You have to be able to say, "I can conquer anything through Christ Jesus."

You should be thinking ahead. You should already be planning for the rest of this year and the beginning of next year. If you wake up every Sunday morning and stand in front of the closet for a half an hour, trying to decide what to wear, you are not a forward thinking person. Sunday happens every week and I am not sure how this is confusing to anyone. It will come next week and the week after that so you should already be prepared.

When I go out to eat at a restaurant, I already know what I am going to order before we even sit down. A lot of times, I can taste my meal before I get to eat it. If you want to be successful in the financial realm, like Donald Trump and others, you have to be a forward thinker. There are too many things to accomplish so I cannot allow people to steal my time. If we want to be successful, these are the attitudes that we have to develop toward how we spend our time.

I realize that there are times when we have to stop and help each other. Galatians 6:2 says to bear one another's burdens. I really don't mind helping. That isn't what I'm talking about. If we are running in the race of life and you trip and break something, I will help you and carry you while you are burdened. If a mom comes in and her husband has left her and she has no money, I will see how I can help her. That is a burden she was not supposed to carry on her own. Christians are supposed to help people with these big burdens so they can get their feet under them and run their race on their own.

But notice that Galatians 6:5 says, "For each shall bear his own load." It is not my job to carry you for the rest of your life. You need to devote your own time to your future.

Part of your load is a job. When you are capable of working, then don't expect me to take care of you. If a guy comes to the church and says, "Hey, I've been out of work for a year and I need some money," I have to say, "Tough. Get a job. I don't know what to tell you, Bro. That is your load. You need to find a job. There are plenty of jobs out there. You may have to work at Burger King for $5 an hour but I guarantee you that I could find six jobs today."

That doesn't mean I won't help when there is a need. That's one of the reasons that I want to be wealthy. Maybe you just got laid off and the bills are piling up. I will help you because that is a burden. I can give you some money to get you through the month, but by next month, you should have a job and be handling your load yourself.

Do not let Satan trick you out of your purpose and destiny by making you feel guilty about not helping others who are too lazy to help themselves. Satan whispers in your ear, "Christians help. You need to give to that person." If there is a genuine need, then give. But if someone just wants to steal your time and your resources, tell them no.

Let's go back to our average guy and see what he could do differently with his time, now that we know how important every minute of the day is to your future and your success. We still have two jars, the wasted jar and the dream jar. We still have twenty-four marbles that represent seeds for the future.

Our guy gets up and he showers and eats breakfast but he changes it up a little. In the shower, he listens to teachings on CD. It might be a teaching on finance or maybe he is listen-

Do not let Satan trick you out of your purpose and destiny.

ing to something that will help him build better relationships. Whatever it is, it helps him to learn and grow and it becomes a seed that brings him closer to his dreams.

After he showers, he eats and reads a few verses out of the Bible, again preparing him for the day and for his future. The first marble of the day goes into the dreams jar.

On the commute to work, he knows that Howard Stern would make such a great impact on his life, but he decides to organize his day or listen to the CD on business management his friend gave him. His commute was productive and he puts another marble in the dreams jar.

He goes to work and while he is there, he works hard the entire time. He does more than the average person. Even when his tasks are menial, he still does his best. He gains favor with his boss and he builds good work habits and a good reputation for the future. A great day of work puts eight marbles in the dreams jar.

His hour lunch was spent meeting with a buddy who talks to him about investments or he reads a great self-help book. That drops another marble in the dreams jar.

Driving home, he listens to a teaching, so he spends an hour gaining knowledge in an area he feels is weak in his life. He puts another marble in the dreams jar.

Our guy goes to the gym with a friend and while they are working out, they discuss different property and land opportunities that they want to invest in the future. So the two hours spent at the gym result in two marbles in his dreams jar.

He has time to relax because no one should spend twenty-four hours learning. You need to give your mind a chance to catch up and process what you have learned during the day. So taking two hours to relax plants marbles in his dream jar.

Then it is time for bed. He gets a good eight hours sleep, which prepares him for the next day. But as he is dozing off to sleep, rather than think of mindless things, he focuses on a problem. It is amazing how many times I have gone to sleep thinking of a problem. My mind worked all night long and when I got up, I had a solution. After eight hours of sleep, he wakes up ready for another successful day.

Instead of twenty-four hours that have done nothing to move him toward his future, our average guy has made every minute count. And now he's not average anymore. Now he is on his way to being part of the elite 5%.

Let me just say that you should not underestimate the value of proper sleep. Sleep is imperative for you to be successful. You need to get eight hours of sleep a night and do not let anyone fool you into thinking otherwise.

You might think that you can get by just fine on five hours. You could run your vehicle on watered down gas, too, and it would work okay for a while but ultimately it would not last as long as it should. It would spit and sputter around and eventually die. Without proper rest, you will limit your overall productivity. Scientifically, we know that you need to have eight hours of sleep or you will cut your life short and limit your abilities.

You have to guard your time, value it and understand the potential it holds for you. When you do, you will find your pace in life that brings you unlimited success. There are so many times we waste our opportunities to learn something and instead, we just space out. At the bank, when you are waiting in line, you can be productive. I can organize my entire week while I am waiting to see a teller and when I get that done, it helps me clear my mind.

Why do successful people use sticky notes and voice recorders throughout the day? They use them because when your mind becomes clogged up thinking of the ten different things you need to get done, it is unable to be creative. You limit your ability to come up with new ideas to solve problems or to produce wealth. When I get an idea, I record it or write it on a sticky note so it is not taking up space in my mind and I can then think about other things and handle current problems. Later, I can go back and read my notes or listen to the recorder and I will remember what I needed with that information. My mind is clear, which allows me to drive down the road thinking about a new sermon or listening to a teaching so I can learn something new and generate new thoughts.

All of this brings us back to the place where we started. If you want to be successful, you have to learn to think the same way that successful people think. You have to think differently about money. You have to think differently about investments. You have to think differently about jobs. You have to think differently about wisdom and the information available to you. You have to think differently about taking risks and you have to think differently about how you manage your time. You have to think differently. If you continue the way you have always gone, you will never make any progress. Change your mind and you will change your future. Start today. Tomorrow depends on it.

On your commitment page, write down, "I will guard my time."

Much may be done in those little shreds and patches of time which every day produces, and which most men throw away.

-Charles Caleb Colton

Be sure to visit LifeWithScot.com for bonus video teachings that are designed to accompany this chapter.

20
STOP CHASING MONEY

*P*eople spend a lifetime chasing the things
*they want, instead create an atmosphere that
attracts the things you want.*

                                        -Scot Anderson

A few years back, I was sitting in a restaurant across
from a guy worth over 500 million dollars. The guy
gave my ministry $5000 to eat with me (funny thing is I
would have paid that to eat with him). This guy proved
yet again that wealthy people think on an entirely different level. At one point, I said my TV ministry required
a lot of money to stay on the air. Right away, he asked
how much was a lot of money. I thought a moment to
gather my latest calculations from my accountant, then
naturally I rounded up a little (sorry, I am human) and
I said $10,000 a week. A look of mixed emotions flit-
tered across his face. It looked like disappointment and
maybe a little pity.

He then smiled and said, "I thought you said it was
a lot. Last week, I shelled out another 20 million dollars
for one of my ventures." I was slightly embarrassed and
taken aback. I then waited the rest of the conversation for
him to say, "Hey let me pick up the tab." These words

never came out of his mouth, and I don't believe ever entered his thoughts.

Later, as I played that over in my head, his reaction made sense to me. He is worth at least 200 times what I am worth. It is like me sitting down with someone whose total net worth is 10k and they say to me they have this big expense that is important to their future. I say "Wow, how much is it?" They reply $50. My mind would be like, *That isn't that big of a deal. You should be able to raise that with very little effort.* I would not even consider helping because it is such a small amount that is definitely reachable by that person. Giving it to them might even hinder their growth and satisfaction from doing it on their own. To him, $10,000 is like pocket change. It's like most people wondering if they should supersize their meal and spend the extra $1.37.

In the conversation that followed he said something to me that was more life changing than everything all the other wealthy people said put together. This one phrase changed my life, and I know for a fact this is how wealthy people at their core think. He said, "People spend their whole life chasing money and never catching it."

Let's stop right there for a moment. Isn't that what we do? We chase that good old dollar. Chase it at work, chase it to retirement, chase it in our budgets, chase it on Wall Street, chase it in our business... Our parents spent their entire lives chasing the same thing our grandparents chased. No one caught it, why do we think we will?

He continued, "People spend their whole life chasing money and never catching it. I decided at a very young age to become someone that attracted money. I want money to chase me." There it is. That might be one of the greatest statements on money ever spoken. We spend our whole life chasing money, when all we need to do is become the person that money chases. There is a huge difference between the guy who has to go beat down doors trying to find a good business deal and the guy who great business deals are beating down his door. There is a huge difference between the guy who spends his whole life looking for money making opportunities and the guy for whom money making opportunities come looking.

Let's think in the terms of deer hunting. Most of us know a deer hunter, been around one, read about one. When I was fourteen years old, my dad took me deer hunting (not one of our great father/son trips). Neither one of us had ever hunted deer, but in our minds it seemed easy. Get a gun, go out in the forest, find a deer, and shoot it. What is sad and maybe funny is we wouldn't have known what to do with it if we did get a deer, which is similar to people and money.

So we go out deer hunting. We wondered around that stupid forest for three days and never saw a deer. Simply put, we were chasing the deer like most people chase money. Later we found out that you don't chase deer, you create an environment that attracts the deer to you. You never hear of a deer hunter training for the deer season. "I have to get in prime shape to catch that deer." There are no classes to get a hunter more speed and agility. Honestly, deer hunters are quite the opposite, they're maybe a little lazy. They spend their time building a huge chair in a tree so they can sit for eight hours at a time. The hunter doesn't prepare to chase the deer, the hunter prepares the environment to attract the deer to him. The hunter gets all the right gear on, gets the perfect spot, and rubs deer pee on themselves. (Who would have thought you could start a business and make millions selling deer pee? Funny question is, how do you know it is deer pee? If you can make millions selling deer pee, that tells me that whatever million dollar idea God has given you, it definitely is a good one.) The hunter creates an environment that brings the deer to them.

This is what I want to talk about. How do we become that person who attracts money? Business deals, money making opportunities, people, ideas come to us. How do we become that person money chases? The Bible says that blessings will run us down. That is what we want! We want blessings beating down our door.

Follow me through the next few scriptures as I show you the secret. Galatians 3:14 and 3:26 say the same covenant Abraham had with God, we have. So what is this covenant? Lets go to Genesis 12:2 to find out. God says, "I will make you a great nation, I will bless you with an abundant increase of favor."

Favor is the key. Favor is better than money. Money comes and goes, but favor attracts money, ideas, businesses to you. To the world, favor is luck. The world says, "Scot is just lucky." No, Scot has the favor of God on him. It is that favor that brought me a toy company. That favor brought me great land deals, brought me book opportunities, gets me best speaking engagements in the biggest churches, and got me on CNN to be co-interviewed with Steve Forbes, and brought me my Internet company. I could go on and on. How do you explain a 5'4" guy stuck with an eighties hair-do getting a gorgeous wife (inside and out)? Favor. There are a lot of single people out there trying to chase Mr./Mrs. Right. Why not become the person that Mr/Mrs Right chases? A deer hunter who chases deer only catches the sick ones. Maybe it is time you stop chasing those sick relationships and tap into the power of favor.

In the next few chapters, we will discuss how to activate the favor of God in your life. I know many Christians believe that just because I am saved I get the favor. If that was true, then all Christians would be blessed. That isn't true. There is a flaw in that thinking. Jesus said if something doesn't work, doesn't produce, then cut it down. It's time to cut that thinking down.

First, let's briefly explain what a covenant is. A covenant is a two-sided thing. Our covenant with God is two sided. When we do our part, God will always do His part. When we don't do our part, then the covenant is broken. Let me give you an example. Me and my kids have a chore covenant. If they do their chores, I will always give them their allowance. I would never go back on that, just like your God would never go back on His end. Let's say Laken comes to me and says, "Dad, I need my allowance," but I know he hasn't done his chores. I would say, "Sorry son, no allowance for you." Now he could sit around and claim his covenant all he wanted, he could name and claim it, he could pray for it, beg for it, but it doesn't matter, he did not keep his end of the covenant. Same thing for our covenant with God. If we will do our part, God will always do His. But if we don't, well then no favor for you.

Luke 2:52 says Jesus grew in favor with God and man. Before Jesus embarked on His purpose, it was important that He grew in favor. Since we are Christ like, we to need to grow in favor. Connect to that covenant, and increase in favor. In the following chapters, we will discuss the ten ways we increase in favor. Don't just read the chapters, but be a doer of the chapters.

Be sure to visit LifeWithScot.com for bonus video teachings that are designed to accompany this chapter

21
KNOW WHAT IS RIGHTFULLY YOURS

I have come so you can have a great, abundandant, happy, fulfilled, exciting life.
-Jesus (Author paraphrased)

Number one: You have to know covenant. What can you have? What can you expect out of life? Most Christians don't know what is their right.

There is a story of a young man who ran away at age sixteen. At age 30, a lawyer found him living on the street, homeless and broke. The lawyer said "Your parents passed away ten years ago, leaving you millions of dollars." Understand this: That man was a millionaire by all definitions for over ten years, yet never enjoyed his wealth. Why? Because he did not know what was rightfully his. As Christians, we have great wealth ready for us. But if we don't know what is rightfully ours, we will go a lifetime not enjoying it.

Let me give you a few scriptures concerning what God wants you to have. The Bible has a lot more scriptures on God's blessings. I encourage you to search them out. Learn them, know them, meditate on them. Faith (what you believe) comes through hearing. Until you truly believe that God wants you blessed, you will subconsciously fight the blessings. Genesis 12:2 showed you that we have the same favor as Abraham. Genesis 24:1 tells us God blessed Abraham in all things (same covenant we have). Romans 8:31 says if God is for me (his favor is on me), who can be against me. Verse 32 continues, He shall freely give us all things (in other words, blessings come to me). First Corinthians 3:21 says all things are ours. First Timothy 6:17 says God gives us richly all things to enjoy. Hebrews 6:13 says after Abraham waited patiently, he received the promise (the same promise we are afforded). Third John 1:2 says God will make you prosper in all things, even in health as your thinking prospers.

That is exciting that all that Abraham had, I can have. You look at Abraham's life and the favor of God was on him. Money seemed to chase him. It didn't matter that his nephew Lot took the best land, the best opportunity, God's favor brought blessings to Abraham, not to Lot. Favor is more powerful than even opportunity, more powerful than what our eye can see. So what if someone else took something that was yours? Favor will bring back a seven times return. So what if your business looks bleak? With favor, even bleak becomes abundant. Whatever Abraham touched seemed to prosper. At the end of his life, he had received all the promises. Isn't that what we want?

It is important to note that there was a process for that thirty-year-old homeless guy mentioned at the beginning of the chapter to get his millions. Same thing for the covenant. There are things we have to do to get our money—knowing we have it available isn't enough. Faith without works is dead. We can't be just hearers of the Word, we have to be doers.

This week:
1. Research blessings scriptures, prosperity scriptures, God's goodness scriptures and write them down.
2. Every morning, read them when you get up.

Be sure to visit LifeWithScot.com for bonus video teachings that are designed to accompany this chapter.

22
FAVOR SOURCE

By reading the scriptures I am so renewed that all nature seems renewed around me and with me. The sky seems to be a pure, a cooler blue, the trees a deeper green. The whole world is charged with the glory of God and I feel fire and music under my feet.

-Thomas Merton

This point is the most important. Without this one, none of the others will matter. In order for us to get Abraham's favor, I feel it is important to look at his life and what he did. Now the Lord had said to Abraham:

Get out of your country,
From your family
And from your father's house,
To a land that I will show you.
I will make you a great nation;
I will bless you
And make your name great;
And you shall be a blessing.
I will bless those who bless you,
And I will curse him who curses you;
And in you all the families of the earth shall be blessed.

(Genesis 12:1-3)

There in verse 3, we find the reason for favor. The reason is the source. The reason God wants you blessed is so you can bless all those around you. Why? To answer this question, we need to talk about what God's purpose is. Purpose dictates design. Why is a lawn mower designed the way it is? Its purpose dictates why it is designed with long handles and a blade on the bottom. Purpose dictates design.

What does God want, what is His purpose? He wants every single person saved, that is what He wants. Up until Abraham God was not getting His desire. Think about the time of Noah. Some say there were 1.2 billion people on the earth at the time of Noah, but only one good person. Honestly, that isn't good numbers. I can see God sitting in the board room going over the numbers. Gabriel is like, "It looks like a recession of good people, but I foresee an upturn. In the next fifty years, we hope to have doubled that number."

Then after Noah, you have the tower of Babel, and finally you get to Abraham. Out of the whole earth, all God has at this time is Abraham, who didn't listen to God in the beginning and most Bible scholars agree had idols. God chose him, not based on his works (same reason for us) but because he believed.

God knew that His only marketing on earth was us. His creation should have showed His power, but simple minded humans started worshiping the creation. God said "I need a people in whom I can show My power. Then the world will look at My blessed people and want Me as their God."

It is like sponsorships. When we watch a great golfer and we see they are wearing Nike, we say we need to wear Nike. The person's success points us to something different in their life. Something they have and we don't. We crave the success, so we begin to wear and use the product. God was the originator of the sponsorship program. God wants your friends, neighbors, work associates, and relatives to see His power and favor working in your life. They will say, "what is different about their life? They aren't smarter than me, not better than me, the only difference is they have God."

God's favor is reserved for those who are glorifying Him. The word "glorify," as I explained earlier, means to make God look bigger. When the pro golfer wins a tournament wearing Nike, he makes Nike look bigger, better. I want you to understand that God's power and His favor are reserved for those who enlarge God. "Well pastor how can I do that in my small life?" Remember if you are faithful in the little, you become ruler over much. If you can make God look big in your small world, God will increase your world.

My parents started out a couple of broke Christians in 1971. They spent their time making God look bigger in all that they did, whether it was working harder at work than anyone else, or acting different around old friends, working on their marriage, or raising great kids. Today, they minister to millions of people a year. God increased their world.

Let's go back to the statement that God's favor is reserved for those who glorify Him. There is a reason why Nike hasn't offered me a sponsorship. On the golf course, I would not make them look bigger, they might even pay me not to wear Nike. Why would God give you blessings if you make God look small, insignificant. But when we make God look big, our life becomes limitless.

Look at your life. Do you make God look big at work? Do you make God look big in your relationships? To your friends? To your relatives? Do people see something different in your life? It doesn't mean you have lots of money. My parents didn't have lots of money in the beginning. But you could look at their life and see something different. From that, God's favor began to bring the blessings into their life.

But indeed for this purpose I have raised you up, that I may show My power in you, and that My name may be declared in all the earth.

(Exodus 9:16)

God wants to show His power and favor in you so that His name can be declared in all the earth. His favor is reserved for those who make Him look big.

Whether you know it or not, people know you are a Christian and they are watching your life. They know something is missing in their life, and they want to see if what you have works. So what do they see when they are watching? Are you negative about life? Can you imagine watching a negative golfer wearing Nike? "I don't think I will do that good in the tournament. Nothing ever goes my way. Just another struggle for me. You know, Nike makes me sick, and sends me problems all the time." Come on. No one would use Nike. Are you lazy at work? God's favor works through the person who gives 110 percent.

Let me leave you with this. Yes, we have the power and favor of God available to us, but we have to plug into that power. You plug in by making God look bigger. You unplug yourself when you make God look smaller. Bible says when we humble ourselves and make God look big, He exalts our life. This means I look small, God looks big.

This week:

1. When you get up, remind yourself that today you will be making God look bigger.
2. While you drive, remind yourself to make God look bigger.
3. Before you go into work, remind yourself to make God look bigger.
4. All day, every day, remind yourself to make God look bigger. Do this until it is in your heart, in your mind, but most importantly it is in your actions.

Be sure to visit LifeWithScot.com for bonus video teachings that are designed to accompany this chapter.

23
GET PLANTED OR DIE

You can be committed to Church but not committed to Christ, but you cannot be committed to Christ and not committed to church.

-Joel Osteen

Lets look at what God first had Abraham do. God told Abraham, "Leave your family and friends and go to a land I will show you." God told him to go and get planted in a land. God wants to show His power and favor through us in a land. He needs people and a place. He needs us planted and grounded in a land. Canaan is a picture of the church. We plug into favor when we are in planted in the church.

Those that are planted in the house of the Lord will flourish.

(Psalm 92:13)

Think of yourself as one of those plants in the plastic bucket at Home Depot. Sure you look pretty good now, but in time if you are not planted, you begin to whither. Not being in the church keeps you from growing, expanding, getting your roots down. You wake up one day and your life seems withered. Your relationships have fallen apart. Life is far below the level you wanted.

The Bible says to work out your salvation, meaning we need to get to the spiritual gym. Go to that trainer (the pastor) and find out what the workout is for the week. Get around other Christians who are working out also. This motivates you. Find out what weak areas you have and focus on them. What happens if you stop working out for six months? You get flabby. It is a slow process that you don't notice until one day you get out of the shower, lean over and a half gallon of water spills out of your belly-button. The same is true for life. We need to work out our life, continue to grow and change. Get around people who are pushing you to greatness, not holding you back. If you're not planted, you are dying.

Studies show Christians have the same divorce rate as the world (50% divorce rate), give or take a percent. Christians who attend church regularly and go to a marriage conference every year have a .0005% divorce rate. Of Christians who are married, only around 20 percent say they are happily married. For Christians who go to church on a regular basis and attend a marriage conference once a year, over 80 percent are happily married. What do you know? God's Word works.

Let's see it from God's perspective. God wants the world saved. His church is where the world should see His people flourishing. Now the world is drawn to His church. Look at what happened to Israel when they got planted in the land.

So the LORD gave to Israel all the land of which He had sworn to give to their fathers, and they took possession of it and dwelt in it. The LORD gave them rest all around, according to all that He had sworn to their fathers. And not a man of all their enemies stood against them; the LORD delivered all their enemies into their hand. Not a word failed of any good thing which the LORD had spoken to the house of Israel. All came to pass.

(Joshua 21:43)

The covenant came to pass, when they were planted. God had told Abraham earlier to go to the land, but Abraham, like most Christians, didn't completely listen to God.

And Terah took his son Abram and his grandson Lot, the son of Haran, and his daughter-in-law Sarai, his son Abram's wife, and they went out with them from Ur of the Chaldeans to go to the land of Canaan; and they came to Haran and dwelt there.

(Genesis 11:31)

They came to Haran and dwelt there. The word "Haran" means halfway. Abraham was halfway to where God wanted him. Now God did nothing for Abraham as long as he was not fully committed. It wasn't until Abraham got grounded, that the favor of God began to work.

How many Christians are halfway in the church? They go a couple of times a month, then they wonder where this power of God is. They may go every week, but they don't take notes, don't grow, don't change. During the service, their mind is on the football game, or what they had at Wendy's yesterday. They don't serve in the church. God says, "If you will first build My house, I will build yours."

"Well pastor, we are too busy right now." Really! My dad left for work Monday-Saturday at 3 am and got home at 7 pm. Two times a week, he installed smoke detectors from 10pm-Midnight. Most people wouldn't even go to church with that schedule. We never missed church. On top of that, my parents ran the childrens ministry for free every week. They spent their life building God's house, and God sure built theirs.

I'm not saying you must be at the church every day, you need balance. But you need to go to at least one service a week, and serve in some area. Give God a few hours a week of service. God says, "What you sow, you will reap." Sow some time, and you will be amazed at how God gives you time in return.

God wants your friends, neighbors, and relatives to see that you are church going people and to see the difference it makes in your life. If you are a Christian and not going to church, how does it do God any good to bless you? God's power is reserved for His glory.

"Well pastor, I know lots of people who go to church all the time and their life isn't blessed." Yes, and I know people who wear Nike who are horrible golfers. You can't just go to church, serve in the church and expect the power. You have to learn, grow, change, and do. There is more than one ingredient in getting God's favor, just like there is more than one ingredient in making a cake. To make a great cake, I have to follow the directions and use all the ingredients. I can't throw some eggs in a bowl with sugar, skip the flour and expect a great cake. Many Christians pick and choose what ingredients of life they want to use and then wonder why the cake of life is no good.

Let me say this. Church is the foundation to having God's favor working in your life.

This week:
1. Go to church, do this every week for ever.
2. Volunteer somewhere in your church.
3. In the next month become a member of your church.
4. Begin to hang out with people in your church, more on that next chapter.

Be sure to visit LifeWithScot.com for bonus video teachings that are designed to accompany this chapter.

24
LOSERS!

He who hangs with a fool, becomes a fool. So stop hanging with those idiots at school.
                                        -My Dad, 1984

Number four is also found in those first instructions given to Abraham.

"Leave your family and friends and go.."
                                        (Genesis 12:1)

The first thing we have to do is get away from the negative influences in our life. God knew that in order for Abraham to step into his favor, he had to get away from all the things pulling him down. Negative people, time stealers, pessimists, victims, and persecutors all hinder the favor of God in your life. They suck the favor out of your life. A negative person cannot attract positive things. It is a fact. You can't be around someone negative and expect positive things to come to you. Proverbs 13:20 says he who walks with the wise becomes wise, those who hang with fools become a fool. Hang with negative, you will become negative. I know I said it earlier in the book, but I want to hit it again because it is so important.

You want to be around people who pull you up, not drag you down. People who push you to do and be more, not those who are jealous when you get more. You want to get around people who want to change themselves, not just change spouses and channels. You want to get around people who want to change the neighborhood, the city, the nation, the world. You don't want big talkers, you want to get around big doers. If I become who I am around, then I need to get around some people who are headed towards success, not headed towards retirement.

Write this next quote down. You will grow to the level of those with whom you choose to associate. Look around you. At what level are your friends and influences? You will never go beyond them. Now if they are growing, wanting more also, then great. But if they are stuck in the same place, then you need to become Abraham.

"Well Pastor, what about them?" They have a choice, they can follow you to success, or they can stay and struggle. I refuse to stay and struggle with them. Their lack of growth will not hinder me from doing all God wants me to do in life. I will not allow another person to hold me back from my purpose and my destiny.

Wrong people negate favor. From a father's perspective, when my kids are hanging with a wrong crowd, it negates my favor. I want my kids to get the most out of life, and the wrong people, I know, will hold them back. God knows the same for you. Your influences in life determine the level of your life.

Ben Franklin said, "Associate with people who enjoy the measure of prosperity you would like to enjoy." Why? Because you begin to think like those you are around. Ben Franklin also said "When two or more people work in a positive way there arises out of that union a power that is greater than the sum of individual power."

*B*e careful the environment you choose, for it will shape you; be careful the friends you choose, for you will become like them.

-W. Clement Stone

Identify negative influences. Ask yourself if being around the person brings you up or brings you down, pushes you to do more or holds you back. Remember you only get one life, why would you want to be held back from making it great.

This week.

1. Make a list of all the people you seem to spend time with.
2. Next to their names, write down if they are a positive influence or negative influence.
3. You know what to do—get around the people who will push you to greatness.

Be sure to visit LifeWithScot.com for bonus video teachings that are designed to accompany this chapter.

25
GIVE YOUR FAVOR AWAY

Words which do not give the light of Christ increase the darkness.

-Mother Teresa

God told Abraham that he would be blessed to be what? To be a blessing. Isn't that I have been saying since the beginning of the book? When touching the world, changing the world, being a blessing to the world is in the forefront of our thinking, we activate the power of God to work in our life. Psalms 35:27 says God gives us wealth to show the world His glory. God wants to get the world saved. We are His only marketing instruments. If we are blessed, then God looks bigger, thus making more people want to get saved. We glorify God, thus plugging into power and favor.

Proverbs 11:24 says "there is one who scatters yet increases more, and there is one who withholds more than is right. But it leads to poverty." The generous soul will be made rich. He who waters will also be watered himself. Proverbs 11:27 says he who earnestly seeks good finds favor, then it goes on to say those that trust in money will fall. See, our trust is in God, knowing that we can't out give God. I can't be too big of a blessing. Yes God wants us to enjoy our blessings, but never at the expense of being a blessing. If you give, if you water, you will be given to. If you withhold, then it is withheld from you.

We need to be people who are actively looking for ways to give, looking for ways to be a blessing. This heart and mindset opens the windows of heaven and puts God's favor on our life. Abraham let Lot have the best land, why? It was all his. He understood the favor of God is not about getting things, but about using our things to be a blessing. If you chase things, then you will spend your life never attaining things. If you spend your life using things to bless others, things will continue to flood your direction.

I have found in life that the biggest activator of favor is love. A heart of love and giving will always touch the heart of God. Let me give you an example. Peyton my youngest son, got this awesome Batman car for his birthday. Right as he opened it, you could tell that Baylor was in love with it. Baylor helped Peyton open it, put it together, and then waited patiently for any turn he could get to play with it.

The next day, my mom took Peyton out to the toy store to get a birthday gift. When Peyton came in with Grandma, I asked what he got. Peyton pulled the same Batman car out of the bag. I said, "You already have that one," to which Peyton replied, "I got this one for Baylor."

As a father, that touched my heart deeply. The next day I took Peyton to the toy store and said, "Whatever you want, get." Peyton got a toy that was three times more expensive. I believe that God does the same for you and me. Remember God looks at the heart, also realize that God's heart is a reflection of yours. If your heart is to give, to bless, then God's heart will be to give and to bless. If your heart is to get, to hold back, then God's is the same.

Love is the quickest way to activate favor, while selfishness is the quickest way to stop favor. If you want favor with your wife, give to her. If you want favor with your boss, give to your boss. If you want to lose favor with man, start taking. Favor is activated through giving.

If being a blessing is not in your agenda don't worry, you won't get the chance because it's not in God's agenda for you either.

"Well pastor, when I get some money I will be a blessing." No! Be a blessing now. God says if you are faithful with a little, God will make you ruler over much. If God can't trust you to give when you have a little, He knows you won't give when you have a lot.

Growing up, we were poor. When I say poor, I mean poor. The gangs in our neighborhood had to take the city bus to do a drive-by shooting. I thought my dad could do a miracle similar to Jesus turning water into wine. My dad could take an empty ketchup bottle over to the sink, shake it up, and come back with a ketchup bottle half full of ketchup. It was a miracle. I didn't know ketchup was supposed to be thick until I got married. In my house you had to carefully tip the ketchup bottle, because the red water was ready to gush onto your plate. We grew up poor. Going out to eat was something we maybe did a couple of times a year. Arby's was a huge night for us. We called it going out for steak. Sometimes we even had enough money to get a French fry with our steak sandwich. We would go and get a single scoop ice cream cone for ten cents. My dream as a kid was one day to get that 20-cent triple scoop. We were poor.

One year I remember overhearing my dad saying he didn't have money for Christmas that year. He said he only had $50. So my dad gave it in the offering. As a kid I was like, "Hey! $50 would buy me a good present." That week, by an act of God, my dad sold a car and made $400. For most people, they would take the miracle and use it all on their Christmas. My parents gave $200 to a single mom and her four kids for Christmas, tithed forty dollars and then spent $150 on our Christmas.

In January, my dad sold a record four cars and made $2000. (Remember the chapter on buying and selling cars? This is where I learned this.) God's blessings followed my dad's giving. If we want the blessings then we will start giving. That is like the farmer saying, "I will plant after I get the harvest." God said, "I will not be mocked, whatever a man sows, he shall reap".

A month after teaching this, I had a lady come up to me. She said she was waiting on a miracle for rent. Well God came through, but she got more than she needed. Rather than using the extra for herself, she helped another lady with her rent. The next week she got an unexpected 30% wage increase. She then said something that stuck with me. She said, "I didn't stop the increase in favor."

I wonder how many of us got a blessing and then hoarded it for ourselves and stopped the increase in favor? We got a blessing, more than we could contain, and we kept it, thus stopping the increase in favor. Instead of getting the Batman car for our brother, we got another goodie for ourself.

This is what I want you to work on: Whenever you get a blessing, I want you to first look to see who you can pass the blessing on to. Wealth is not his who has it, but his who joyfully shares it.

Let me add this and I won't talk much about it because we all know it. If you do not tithe, you will not have favor. Sorry, it is true. You can make all the excuses and twist scriptures around all you want. The fact is simple: If you do not tithe, you stop favor from working in your life.

This week:

1. Pass on one blessing to someone else.
2. Now work towards doing this on a daily basis until it becomes who you are. You are someone who is truly blessed to be a blessing.
3. Tithe

Next week:

   1. Tithe

All weeks after:

   1. Tithe

Be sure to visit LifeWithScot.com for bonus video teachings that are designed to accompany this chapter

26

I'D LIKE TO ORDER A PERSON OF GREAT CHARACTER WITH A SIDE OF SELF-CONTROL

Industry, thrift and self-control are not sought because they create wealth, but because they create character.

-Calvin Coolidge

L uke 2:52 says Jesus grew in wisdom and in character.

Your character determines favor. Character is what you are made of, who you really are. Every great man in the Bible who was blessed, you can see they had great character. This doesn't mean they didn't make mistakes, we all do. But they were men and woman of character. Joseph, Abraham, David, Joshua, Daniel, Elijah, Paul, all of them.

Once again, let's go back to the subject of glory. You represent God, your actions make God look big or small. God's power is reserved for His glory. If you lack character, you make God look small and He pulls His sponsorship. Tiger Woods lost a lot of money after the world found out about all his extra-marital affairs. He lost his sponsorship because of his lack of character and how the world viewed him. Your actions say something to the world. If you make God look big, you plug into the power small and you unplug yourself.

I love this quote. "Be careful of thoughts, they become words; careful of words, they become actions; careful of actions, they become habits; careful of habits, they become character; careful of character, it becomes your destiny."

Your character determines the level of your life. Psalm 92:12 says those that have good character flourish.

I wish I had time to detail what good character is. Like many things, you need to get some books and read about it. Learn the virtues and become a person of great character. I personally believe that if you follow two simple rules, you will become a person of great character. First, go after the master virtue which is wisdom and understanding. Wisdom and understanding will teach you who to be and what to do. The pursuit of wisdom and understanding is another reason to be in church, taking notes. Also to be in the word of God daily. Number two, always walk in love. Jesus said, "Let me sum up what life is all about, it is about loving God, loving others, and loving yourself." A person of character is a person who loves God, others, and himself.

Self-control activates favor. God wants to be able to trust you with His blessings. He doesn't want to give His blessings to someone who lacks self-control. The Bible says that those who walk in the Spirit bring life (God's blessings and favor), those who walk in the flesh (lack self-control) bring death (separation from God's blessings and favor).

Did you know that to be happy you have to be in control? You were made to have dominion, to be in control. When you lack self-control, or as I say when something controls you, you have no ability to be happy. The amount of self-control you have will determine the level of life you experience in the future. It's time to control yourself, take charge of your life. Don't allow anything to control you. I am a man of no habits, I refuse to let anything tell me what to do. I live a life of self-control. The Bible says a man who lacks self-control will live a broken life. To me that sounds like a life lacking favor. Take charge of your life, charge of your thoughts, charge of your actions. Take your life back from anything that has a power over you. In my book *Millionaire Habits* I really cover this in detail, I give you some real steps in developing right habits. I encourage you to pick this book up.

We all have dreams, but in order to make dreams a reality it takes determination, dedication, self-discipline, and effort.

This week:

1. Write down a description of the person you want to be. Be very detailed. A person who has a very clear and concise idea of who they want to be will become that person much faster than someone who has a broad sense.

2. Write down a description of the person you are in relation to who you want to be.

3. What do you need to do to become what you want to be. To many people want money, but they don't want to become the person who attracts money. They want a great marriage, but they don't want to become the person who has a great marriage.

4. Now become that person.

Be sure to visit LifeWithScot.com for bonus video teachings that are designed to accompany this chapter.

27

FAVOR NEVER FOLLOWS BAD ATTITUDE

Weakness of attitude becomes weakness of character.

-Albert Einstein

Let's talk about attitude. What is the one thing that kept that first generation of Isrealites out of Promise Land? Attitude. Favor will never follow bad attitude. Faith, positive expectations, and a positive attitude attracts success. You will always get what you expect. If you expect less than, guess what, you will always get less than. If you always see the problem, then the problem will stop you from getting the blessing. We need to be like David, who didn't see the giant, he saw how God could overcome the giant. He said, "Who is this uncircumcised man who comes against the living God." He told his problem that he was going to chop his head off. He ran towards his problem. The rest of Israel sat around whining and complaining, seeing only the problem. David saw that with God all things are possible.

Your attitude determines the amount of favor you will have. If you think you are going nowhere, well you will go nowhere. But if you believe that God is making a way, that He is clearing a path, He is bringing down those Jericho walls, well guess what, the walls are coming down.

Wealthy minded people believe that all things are possible. Since we know God, we should know without a doubt that it is true. To activate favor, you must have a positive attitude. This means you have to have positive thoughts. The Bible says to capture any thought that is negative. I like the word "capture," it is aggressive. You should get mad at any thought of can't. It then says to make that thought obedient to the Word of God. You make it obey. You force it to line up. You have a thought that says you can't, you make it say you can. You have a thought that says you're not smart enough, you make it remember that you have the mind of Christ.

When I was a kid, I dreamed about horseback riding. I loved the western shows and the cowboys on their horses. We were poor so that opportunity didn't come until I was 12. Now my dad grew up in the backwoods of Wisconsin and had been riding a horse since he was probably born. So he knew horses. I thought I knew horses. I had watched enough westerns to know you say giddyup, shake the reigns to go, and pull back to stop.

So I get on my horse and I click my tongue and give the horse a nudge to go forward. My stupid horse turns around and goes in the opposite direction to the corner of the corral. No matter what I did, he just sat there going to the bathroom. Finally, my dad came over and said, "What are you doing?"

I said, "The stupid horse won't do what I want." To which my dad said, "Grab the reins, jerk them, and show that horse who is boss." So I did.

That horse took off. When I wanted to go left, I had to jerk the reins to the left. When right, I jerked the reigns to the right. In just a few minutes something amazing happened. I had to just lightly pull the reins to the left or right to get the horse to turn.

I said all that to say this. For many of you your thoughts are sitting over in the corner refusing to see what you need to do is take those thoughts by the reins and jerk them to where they need to be. A thought comes in your head that you can't do something, you say, "I CAN DO ALL THINGS THROUGH CHRIST THAT STRENGTHENS ME." You have a thought that says you are not smart enough, "I HAVE THE MIND OF CHRIST!" You have a thought that tries to make you remember the past, "I FORGET THOSE THINGS BEHIND ME AND PRESS FORWARD TO THE PRIZE AHEAD!" The Bible says that the battle is not out there somewhere, but it is in our mind for pulling down strongholds and every thought that is contrary to God's Word. We need to capture our thought and make it obedient. That is what I am saying. Capture those thoughts and make them obedient to God's Word. Don't allow your mind to think even one thought that is negative.

*M*ake every thought, every fact, that comes into your mind pay you a profit. Make it work and produce for you. Think of things not as they are but as they might be. Don't merely dream - but create!

-Robert Collier

I love that quote. Put your thoughts to work, make them pay you a profit. A wealthy man once told me that every thought was like a seed. My seeds will make up my garden of life. His question was then, what type of garden are you planting? That changed my life. I wanted a flourishing garden. I don't want one single weed of negativity in there. If you ever had a garden, you know how one weed can spread and cause havoc in your garden. Just one negative thought, just one thought about the past failures can hinder your garden.

Favor is reserved for those who may not know what tomorrow holds, but they know that God holds their tomorrow. Favor is for those who know that God's blessing are coming, and that through God, all things are possible. Favor is for those who are like David, who scoff at their problems no matter how big they are because they know that at the end of the battle, the head of the enemy will lie at their feet.

Your attitude determines how much favor you get.

This week:

1. Set your mind in the morning. Get up and tell yourself this will be an awesome, blessed day.

2. Stop saying what you have, say what you want. If you do that, in time you will have what you say. What I mean is when someone says, "How are you?" Stop saying "I'm okay/I'm alright/things could be better." No more. Say, "I am awesome." "I am blessed." "Life is amazing." Even if that is not currently true, say it long enough and it will be true.

3. Don't allow even one negative thought. Remember every thought is a seed, plant what you want, not what you got. Make your thoughts work for you.

4. Remember this quote my dad always said to me. Don't worry about the harvest of today, instead worry about what you are planting today." Sure life may be hard now, but if I stop worrying about the harvest and start planting right thoughts and actions today, my harvest in the future will be a lot better.

Be sure to visit LifeWithScot.com for bonus video teachings that are designed to accompany this chapter.

28

THANK GOD FOR FAVOR

*E*very *morning I wake up and thank God.*
-Aaron Neville

Be grateful. The Bible says we enter into God's courts with thanksgiving. Thanksgiving keeps the favor coming.

I think many Christians stop the flow of favor because they don't give God the thanks and the credit for the favor. Let me say it again. God's favor and power is reserved for his glory. Let me give you an example. Say God's favor is on you and you get a promotion at work that was unexpected. To yourself you think, *Thank You so much God.* (this is good). Now in the breakroom some co-workers are like, "How did you get that promotion?" You think for a moment, don't want to be embarrassed so you say, "I worked hard, had a little luck go my way, things just worked out." Now did you make God look bigger? So God gives you favor and you take the credit. If I was God I would be like, "So you did it on your own? Okay, I guess you don't need My help." That makes sense.

I believe it is more important to God (because of His purpose of having the world see His power through you) if you said, "It was all God. His favor is on me." Sure your co-workers may roll their eyes or may say something sarcastic. But, a seed was planted. What if that one statement helped that one co-worker come to Christ?

This is something I struggled with and didn't even know it. In my life I am almost always surrounded by Christians, so giving God glory is easy. But the few times a day I am not around Christians, I tended to take the glory for myself, not wanting to act religious. I had to come to grips with the fact that I am not acting religious, I am giving God the glory.

If I bought my kids a bike and I overheard them talking to their friends about how they saved up and got it on their own, that would kind of hurt my feelings. A little part of me wants their friends to see me as a good dad. Now for the sake of the example, let's say that my goal was to get their friends in my family. Now how much more important does it become that they give me the glory, make me look like a great dad?

God showed me how I was taking the glory at the most important times. Who cares if my son Baylor tells my son Peyton that I got him the bike? Peyton would be like, "Of course he did, that is what dads do." It is more important that Baylor tells his friends what I do for him.

I changed this quickly. God recently blessed me with the house of my dreams. I mean this house has things I wanted in a house 20 years ago but forgot and gave up on. Well, when you get a new house, the wife wants new furniture. So I'm Craig's Listing our old stuff. The first lady to come out said, "Your house is amazing." I paused for a moment and almost said my normal, "Thanks." I switched gears and said, "God always seems to bless me." The lady was slightly taken back, then smiled and we went back to business. I believe I planted a seed.

I recently bumped into a few old high school friends who said, "I saw your books in the bookstore, you failed English."

"Yes, I can't write, but God sure can write through me," I responded. They laughed and made a couple sarcastic comments. But in that moment I planted an idea in their hearts. A guy who has no English skills at all is a best selling author. It has to be God.

What do you tell your relatives when they say things about your life? Are you too embarrassed or do you give God the glory? The favor God gives is to make Him look bigger. If you want to keep the flow of favor, then give God the glory.

This week:

1. Remind yourself that God is the source of your blessings throughout the day.

2. Each day give God the glory at least once to one person who is not saved.

3. Every time you are blessed small or big, give God the glory. Make it a habit to let the world know that your God is an amazing God.

Be sure to visit LifeWithScot.com for bonus video teachings that are designed to accompany this chapter.

*B*eing *forced to work, and forced to do your best, will breed in you temperance and self-control, diligence and strength of will, cheerfulness and content, and a hundred virtues which the idle will never know.*

-Charles Kingsley

I f a pro golfer who was sponsored by Nike started showing up late, not practicing, quitting the tournament a few holes early, playing on Facebook during the tournament, basically just giving a half effort, how long would Nike continue to sponsor him?

My God is a God of excellence. He is a God whose favor flows only through excellence. He doesn't like second best (as Cain found out). God wants you to do everything as if you are doing it unto Him. Of course it all comes back to glory. The golfer makes Nike look bigger when he gives his all. You make God look bigger when you give your all.

"Well pastor, I'm in a job that is below me, or in a position not using my gifts." I can tell you that Joseph was not called to be a slave. His gift was not to be the head of a prison. Joseph made it so his boss's only worry in life was what to eat. Is this your attitude at work? Or are you like everyone else who is annoyed because the boss isn't doing anything, annoyed because the boss is late? Your job is to make sure he has nothing to do. Your job is to make sure his only concern is what to order from Subway that day. ·

When you do something, do it as if doing it for God. In a sense you are. People know you are a Christian, what you give is a representation of God. You either glorify God, or you don't. Let's say it again, God's favor is reserved for His glory. Make God look big, and He makes your life big.

Giving your best has to be a lifestyle. Give your best to your spouse, to work, to your church, to God. Isn't this love? Remember, love is one of the biggest activators of favor. I am loving my boss when I work harder than anyone else. I am loving my spouse when I give only my best to the relationship. Favor flows through excellence.

This week:
1. Show up early for work and stay late.
2. Every day do one thing for your boss that is not in your job description
3. Become a I can do it person. When boss is looking for a volunteer, it is you.
4. When you walk from place to place at your job walk faster than anyone. This gives the impression that you hustle.

5.Focus on doing your best at what ever task is at hand. Remind yourself before, during, and after that you are a person of excellence. Work as if what you are doing, you will be turning it in for God to look at.

Be sure to visit LifeWithScot.com for bonus video teachings that are designed to accompany this chapter.

CLOSING THOUGHTS

I know you enjoyed this book. Rember that when you read a book you only retain about 25%, that is why it is important that you complete the workbook. Now you will retain about 50%. If you read the book again and watch the videos, you will retain nearly 90%. I know that you are not a person who wants to do things just halfway, you are someone who is all in. You give 110% in everything you do. Read this book again, watch the videos, do the workbook, and then go do it.

What is the use of having the answer if you don't use it? Go create the environment that will attract blessings to you.

Your friend,

Scot

THINK LIKE A
BILLIONAIRE

BECOME A
BILLIONAIRE

AS A MAN THINKS, SO IS HE

WORKBOOK

THIS
VISION

BELONGS TO

_____

NAME

_____

PHONE

THIS VISION WAS BIRTHED

_____

DATE

Whatever is born of God
overcomes the world.
(1 John 5:4)

God has given you
the power to obtain wealth.
(Deuteronomy 8:18)

WHERE ARE YOU GOING?

Write the vision and make it plain on tablets. (Habakkuk 2:2)

MY GIVING VISION: One day I will give . . .

*But seek first the kingdom of God and His righteousness,
and all these things shall be added to you. (Matthew 6:33)*

Annual Tithe: $_____

```
┌─────────────────────────────────────────────────────┐
│ Future tithe check                                    │
│                          Date _____      0001      │
│                                                       │
│ Pay to the                                            │
│ order of _____  $ [      ] │
│                                                       │
│ Memo _____         _____       │
└─────────────────────────────────────────────────────┘
```

Annual Offering: $_____

```
┌─────────────────────────────────────────────────────┐
│ Future check to charity                               │
│ for annual offering      Date _____      0002      │
│                                                       │
│ Pay to the                                            │
│ order of _____  $ [      ] │
│                                                       │
│ Memo _____         _____       │
└─────────────────────────────────────────────────────┘
```

Total Net Worth Vision: $_____

Do not stop short on this vision. Once you get a million dollars, getting to a billion can be quickly done using some of the same principles that got you the million.

```
┌─────────────────────────────────────────────────────────┐
│ Future check to yourself                                  │
│                             Date _____        0003     │
│                                                           │
│                                                           │
│  Pay to the                                               │
│  order of _____  $ [          ]    │
│                                                           │
│  Memo _____    _____      │
└─────────────────────────────────────────────────────────┘
```

VISION OF GIFTS

List special gifts you would like to give
to a ministry or God's work.
Example: Million Bibles to India

1. _____

2. _____

3. _____

4. _____

5. _____

GIFTS FROM GOD

Desires of Your Heart

Delight yourself also in the LORD,
And He shall give you the desires of your heart.
(Psalm 37:4)

Picture of Desire	*Picture of Desire*
Picture of Desire	*Picture of Desire*

COMMITMENT

He is a double-minded man, unstable in all his ways. (James 1:8)

I,_____, on _____
　　　　　Name　　　　　　　　　　　　Date

am making a commitment to change what is in me, thus changing the life coming out of me. I will begin to think like a billionaire. I will begin to have God's thoughts so I can have His ways. I will change what is in my heart so I can change what comes into my life.

I am committed to each thing I list below (You will get a list of commitments in the book):

1. _____
2. _____
3. _____
4. _____
5. _____
6. _____
7. _____
8. _____
9. _____
10. _____
11. _____
12. _____
13. _____
14. _____
15. _____
16. _____

_____　　_____
　　　Name　　　　　　　　　　　Date

BLESSINGS JOURNAL

Enter into His gates with thanksgiving,
And into His courts with praise. (Psalm 100:4)

Each week, take time to write out the blessings God has given you.
Now each week, also take time to praise God and be thankful.

_____

_____

_____

_____

_____

_____

_____

_____

_____

_____

_____

_____

_____

_____

_____

Initial each week you do this.

___ ___ ___ ___ ___ ___ ___ ___ ___ ___ ___

___ ___ ___ ___ ___ ___ ___ ___ ___ ___ ___

___ ___ ___ ___ ___ ___ ___ ___ ___ ___ ___

BLESSINGS JOURNAL (CONT.)

_____

_____

_____

_____

_____

_____

_____

_____

_____

_____

_____

_____

_____

_____

_____

_____

_____

_____

_____

_____

_____

_____

_____

_____

_____

_____

_____

JOURNAL OF LIFE LESSONS
LEARNING TO FAIL FORWARD

*My brethren, count it all joy when you fall into various trials,
knowing that the testing of your faith produces patience .
But let patience have its perfect work, that you may be
perfect and complete, lacking nothing. (James 1:2-4)*

What happened: _____

_____

_____

_____

_____

_____

_____

_____

What you learned: _____

_____

_____

_____

_____

_____

_____

What you will do next time: _____

_____

_____

_____

_____

_____

_____

JOURNAL OF LIFE LESSONS
LEARNING TO FAIL FORWARD

My brethren, count it all joy when you fall into various trials,
knowing that the testing of your faith produces patience .
But let patience have its perfect work, that you may be
perfect and complete, lacking nothing. (James 1:2-4)

What happened: _____

_____

_____

_____

_____

_____

_____

_____

What you learned: _____

_____

_____

_____

_____

_____

_____

_____

What you will do next time: _____

_____

_____

_____

_____

_____

_____

_____

JOURNAL OF LIFE LESSONS
LEARNING TO FAIL FORWARD

My brethren, count it all joy when you fall into various trials,
knowing that the testing of your faith produces patience .
But let patience have its perfect work, that you may be
perfect and complete, lacking nothing. (James 1:2-4)

What happened: _____

_____

_____

_____

_____

_____

_____

_____

What you learned: _____

_____

_____

_____

_____

_____

_____

_____

What you will do next time: _____

_____

_____

_____

_____

_____

_____

_____

JOURNAL OF LIFE LESSONS
LEARNING TO FAIL FORWARD

*My brethren, count it all joy when you fall into various trials,
knowing that the testing of your faith produces patience .
But let patience have its perfect work, that you may be
perfect and complete, lacking nothing. (James 1:2-4)*

What happened: _____

_____

_____

_____

_____

_____

_____

What you learned: _____

_____

_____

_____

_____

_____

_____

_____

What you will do next time: _____

_____

_____

_____

_____

_____

_____

JOURNAL OF LIFE LESSONS
LEARNING TO FAIL FORWARD

My brethren, count it all joy when you fall into various trials,
knowing that the testing of your faith produces patience .
But let patience have its perfect work, that you may be
perfect and complete, lacking nothing. (James 1:2-4)

What happened: _____

_____

_____

_____

_____

_____

_____

_____

What you learned: _____

_____

_____

_____

_____

_____

_____

What you will do next time: _____

_____

_____

_____

_____

_____

_____

JOURNAL OF LIFE LESSONS
LEARNING TO FAIL FORWARD

My brethren, count it all joy when you fall into various trials,
knowing that the testing of your faith produces patience .
But let patience have its perfect work, that you may be
perfect and complete, lacking nothing. (James 1:2-4)

What happened: _____

_____

_____

_____

_____

_____

_____

_____

What you learned: _____

_____

_____

_____

_____

_____

_____

_____

What you will do next time: _____

_____

_____

_____

_____

_____

_____

_____

JOURNAL OF LIFE LESSONS
LEARNING TO FAIL FORWARD

My brethren, count it all joy when you fall into various trials,
knowing that the testing of your faith produces patience .
But let patience have its perfect work, that you may be
perfect and complete, lacking nothing. (James 1:2-4)

What happened: _____

_____

_____

_____

_____

_____

_____

What you learned: _____

_____

_____

_____

_____

_____

_____

_____

What you will do next time: _____

_____

_____

_____

_____

_____

_____

JOURNAL OF LIFE LESSONS
LEARNING TO FAIL FORWARD

My brethren, count it all joy when you fall into various trials,
knowing that the testing of your faith produces patience .
But let patience have its perfect work, that you may be
perfect and complete, lacking nothing. (James 1:2-4)

What happened: _____

_____

_____

_____

_____

_____

_____

_____

What you learned: _____

_____

_____

_____

_____

_____

_____

_____

What you will do next time: _____

_____

_____

_____

_____

_____

_____

JOURNAL OF LIFE LESSONS
LEARNING TO FAIL FORWARD

My brethren, count it all joy when you fall into various trials,
knowing that the testing of your faith produces patience .
But let patience have its perfect work, that you may be
perfect and complete, lacking nothing. (James 1:2-4)

What happened: _____

_____

_____

_____

_____

_____

_____

What you learned: _____

_____

_____

_____

_____

_____

_____

What you will do next time: _____

_____

_____

_____

_____

_____

_____

JOURNAL OF LIFE LESSONS
LEARNING TO FAIL FORWARD

My brethren, count it all joy when you fall into various trials,
knowing that the testing of your faith produces patience .
But let patience have its perfect work, that you may be
perfect and complete, lacking nothing. (James 1:2-4)

What happened: _____

_____

_____

_____

_____

_____

_____

_____

What you learned: _____

_____

_____

_____

_____

_____

_____

_____

What you will do next time: _____

_____

_____

_____

_____

_____

_____

_____

DAILY CONFESSION

*Faith comes by hearing and hearing and hearing
and hearing the Word of God. (Romans 10:17, paraphrased)*

2 Corinthians 1:20
I am blessed.

Genesis 12:3
God will bless those who bless me and curse those who curse me.

Genesis 12:3
I am a blessing to all the peoples of the earth.

Genesis 15:1
Lord, I am not afraid, for You are my shield and my very great reward.

Genesis 18:18
I have received all the blessings of Abraham in Christ. I will surely become a great and powerful nation and all nations on earth will be blessed through me.

Genesis 24:35
The Lord has blessed me abundantly and I have become wealthy.

Genesis 26:12
I planted seed and the same year reaped a hundredfold because the Lord has blessed me.

Deuteronomy 1:11
Thank You, God, for increasing me a thousand times and blessing me as You have promised.

Deuteronomy 7:13
You love me, Lord; You bless me and increase me.

Deuteronomy 28:2
The blessings come upon me and overtake me.

Deuteronomy 28:4
All my possessions are blessed.

Deuteronomy 28:6
I am blessed when I go in and blessed when I come out.

Deuteronomy 28:7
The Lord will grant that the enemies who rise up against me are defeated before me. The enemy comes in one direction and flees from me in seven.

Deuteronomy 28:8
The Lord sends blessings on everything I put my hand to. The Lord blesses me in the land He has given me.

Deuteronomy 28:11
The Lord has granted me abundant prosperity.

Deuteronomy 28:12
The Lord has opened the heavens, the storehouse of His bounty, to bless all the work of my hands.

Deuteronomy 28:13
The Lord has made me the head and not the tail. I am always at the top and never at the bottom.

Psalm 34:9
I fear the Lord and lack nothing.

Psalm 1:2-3
My delight is in the law of the Lord. On Your law I meditate day and night. I am like a tree planted by streams of water which yields its fruit in season and whose leaf does not wither. Whatever I do prospers.

Deuteronomy 8:18
Thank you, God, for You have given me the ability to produce wealth and so confirm Your covenant which You swore to my forefathers.

Psalm 25:13
I spend my days in prosperity and my descendants will inherit the land.

Psalm 72:7
I am the righteous and I am flourishing; I have abounding prosperity until the moon is no more.

Psalm 112:1
I am blessed because I fear the Lord and I find great delight in God's commands.

Psalm 112:3
Wealth and riches are in my house.

Psalm 128:1-2
I fear the Lord and walk in His ways. I eat the fruit of my labor. Blessings and prosperity will be mine.

Proverbs 8:17-18
I love You, Lord, and You love me. I seek You and find You. With You are riches and honor, enduring wealth and prosperity.

Malachi 3:10-11
I bring You the whole tithe into the storehouse that there is food in Your house. You, Lord Almighty, have thrown open the floodgates of heaven and poured out so much blessing that I do not have room enough for it. Lord, You rebuke the devourer for my sake so that he will not destroy the fruit of my ground, nor shall the vine fail to bear fruit for me in the field, says the Lord of hosts.

Proverbs 10:22
I have received the blessing of the Lord that has brought me wealth, and He adds no trouble to it.

Proverbs 11:25
I am a generous person. I will prosper.

Proverbs 13:21
I have received the righteousness of Christ. Prosperity is my reward.

Proverbs 21:21
I have pursued righteousness and love. I have found life, prosperity and honor.

Proverbs 22:4
I have received the humility of Christ, and the fear of the Lord has brought me wealth and honor and life.

Ecclesiastics 5:19
God, You have given me wealth and possessions and enabled me to enjoy them, to accept my lot and be happy at my work—this is a gift from You.

Ephesians 1:3
God has blessed me in the heavenly realms with every spiritual blessing in Christ.

Psalm 20:4
God, You grant me according to my heart's desire and fulfill all my purposes.

Proverbs 13:12
When my desires are fulfilled, it is a tree of life to me.

Psalm 103:5
God, You satisfy my desires with good things so that my youth is renewed like the eagle's.

Psalm 37:4
I delight myself in You, Lord, and You will give me the desires of my heart.

Psalm 21:2-3
You have given me my heart's desire, and have not withheld the request of my lips. For You meet me with the blessings of goodness; You set a crown of pure gold upon my head.

Psalm 145:16
You open Your hand and satisfy the desire of every living thing.

Psalm 145:19
God, You will fulfill my desires, for I fear you.

Proverbs 10:24
My desires will be granted; for I am righteous.

Ephesians 3:20
Now to You, God, who is able to do exceedingly abundantly above all that I ask or think, according to the power that works in me.

Proverbs 13:4
I am diligent and my desires are fully satisfied.

Philippians 4:19
My God shall supply all my needs.

3 John 2
I prosper in all things, even health, just as my soul prospers.

Psalm 35:27
For the Lord has pleasure in my prosperity.

Deuteronomy 28:11
The Lord shall make me plenteous in goods, in the fruit of my body, and in the fruit of my cattle, and in the fruit of my ground.

Deuteronomy 28:8
The Lord shall command the blessing upon me in all that I set my hand to.

Matthew 6:33
I seek first the expansion of God's kingdom worldwide, and all these things shall be added unto me.

Psalm 84:11
No good thing will He withhold from me whose walk is upright.

Psalm 112:1-3
Blessed am I who fears the Lord, who delights greatly in His commandments. Wealth and riches shall be in my house.

Psalm 28:20
I am a faithful person and abound with blessings.

Psalm 68:19
Blessed is the Lord, who daily loads me with benefits.

Deuteronomy 29:9
I keep the words of this covenant that I may prosper in all that I do.

Ecclesiastics 5:19
Riches and wealth are the gift of God.

Deuteronomy 28:12
The Lord will open to me His good treasure.

1 Kings 2:3
I walk in His ways that I may prosper in all I do and wherever I turn myself.

John 10:10
Jesus came that I may have life, and that I may have it more abundantly.

Proverbs 8:17, 18, 21
I seek the Lord early and find Him. Riches and honor are with the Lord; yes, durable riches and righteousness that He may cause me, who loves Him, to inherit substance; and He will fill my treasures.

This week, I confessed these scriptures (initial):

___ ___ ___ ___ ___ ___ ___ ___ ___ ___ ___

___ ___ ___ ___ ___ ___ ___ ___ ___ ___ ___

___ ___ ___ ___ ___ ___ ___ ___ ___ ___ ___

___ ___ ___ ___ ___ ___ ___ ___ ___ ___ ___

SELF-CONTROL
ANOTHER WORD FOR BUDGET

A man without self-control is as defenseless
as a city with broken-down walls. (Proverbs 25:28, paraphrased)

Your credit card statement each month reflects the amount of self-control you had in your past. Too many of us spend tomorrow's money on desires for today. Then one day we don't have money for today because we spent it and paid interest on it yesterday.

There is one who makes himself rich,
yet has nothing.
(Proverbs 13:7)

The most important part of this budget is self-control. Without self-control, this budget is useless. If you and your family can't live within your means, after a while, your means won't even cover your needs.

With this budget, there may be a season when you have to do without, because you spent today's money yesterday. I do promise that with this budget, you will have security in knowing where you are headed. You will know you have money for Christmas, vacation, your bills, etc. I also believe you will be headed toward a bright financial future, because you are paying off debt faster than you are accumulating it.

This is not like most budgets you have seen or have tried before. Most of us in the past have said, "Okay, my house is $500, car is $300, insurance is $100, groceries are $200, spending is $200, gas is $100, credit cards are $150, electricity is $100 and water is $50.

"Okay, I make $2,000 a month. My bills are $1,700. So I have an extra $300 a month to spend on whatever I want (clothes, music, going out . . .)."

Then comes birthdays, Christmas, Valentines, anniversaries, vacation, car registration . . . Since you already spent that $300 a month, you now have to swipe the MasterCard. Lack of planning at the end of the year has caused your credit card payoff to increase thousands of dollars.

This budget is designed to cover every single expense you will incur this year and budget your money so you have the money when the time comes.

MY BUDGET

Income:
Monthly (Take Home) Salary = Weekly x 4.3333
(Use the amount you take home after taxes)

_____

Expenses:
Absolutes (Monthly Amount): These amounts are
what you have to pay each month no matter what.

Tithe: (.10 x monthly salary)   _____

Offering   _____

Investment Money (Seed: .10 x monthly salary)   _____

House Payment or Rent   _____

Automobile   _____

Automobile   _____

Auto Insurance   _____

Cable TV   _____

Homeowner's Fees   _____

Life Insurance   _____

Credit Card (_____)   _____

Credit Card (_____)   _____

Credit Card (_____)   _____

Credit Card (_____)   _____

Bank Charges   _____

Additional (_____)   _____

Additional (_____)   _____

Additional (_____)   _____

Total of Absolutes: _____

BUDGET (CONT.)

Absolutes Estimated (Monthly):

These are amounts you have to pay, but the
amount varies. Do your best to estimate.

Auto Gas _____

Electricity _____

Cell Phone _____

Medical Expenses (Co-pays & Prescription Costs) _____

Dental _____

Eye (Glasses and Exams) _____

City (Garbage and Water) _____

Telephone _____

Groceries _____

Total of Absolutes Estimated: _____

Yearly Absolutes:	**Yearly**		**Monthly**
Education	_____	÷ 12 =	_____
Automobile Registration	_____	÷ 12 =	_____
Maintenance	_____	÷ 12 =	_____
(4 oil changes, etc.)			

Total of Yearly Absolutes Monthly Amount: _____

BUDGET (CONT.)

Personal and Family (Monthly):
Things you want and must fit within your budget.
(These amounts may have to be adjusted in order to balance your budget.)

Clothing Me   _____

Clothing Spouse   _____

Clothing Kid   _____

Clothing Kid   _____

Clothing Kid   _____

Personal Spending, Me   _____

Personal Spending, Spouse   _____

Kids' Allowances   _____

Kids' Lunches   _____

Kids' Programs (Sports, piano, etc.)   _____

Auto Wash and Extras   _____

Childcare   _____

Dry-Cleaning   _____

Spending (Out to eat, movies, etc.)   _____

Home Upgrades   _____

Haircut, Me   _____

Haircut, Spouse   _____

Haircut, Kids   _____

Nails and Makeup   _____

Miscellaneous   _____
    (Very important. I have 2% of my monthly
    income here for those things that I forgot about)

Children Miscellaneous   _____

Total Personal and Family   _____

BUDGET (CONT.)

Yearly Miscellaneous:

These amounts may have to be adjusted in order to balance your budget.

Christmas Family (List name and amount)

_____ + _____ + _____

_____ + _____ + _____

_____ + _____ + _____

	Yearly	**Monthly**
Total Family Christmas	_____ ÷ 12 =	_____

Christmas Friends (List name and amount)

_____ + _____ + _____

_____ + _____ + _____

_____ + _____ + _____

	Yearly	**Monthly**
Total Friends Christmas	_____ ÷ 12 =	_____
Christmas people you don't like but you have to give a gift	_____ ÷ 12 =	_____
Christmas Tree	_____ ÷ 12 =	_____
Christmas Decorations	_____ ÷ 12 =	_____
Christmas Miscellaneous	_____ ÷ 12 =	_____
Anniversary	_____ ÷ 12 =	_____
Valentines Day	_____ ÷ 12 =	_____

BUDGET (CONT.)

Birthday Family (List name and amount)

_____ + _____ + _____

_____ + _____ + _____

_____ + _____ + _____

	Yearly	**Monthly**
Total Family Birthday	_____ ÷ 12 =	_____

Birthday Friends (List name and amount)

_____ + _____ + _____

_____ + _____ + _____

_____ + _____ + _____

	Yearly	**Monthly**
Total Friends Birthday	_____ ÷ 12 =	_____
Gifts (Weddings, Baby Showers)	_____ ÷ 12 =	_____
Vacation	_____ ÷ 12 =	_____

Total of Yearly Miscellaneous: _____

BUDGET (CONT.)

Time to find out if your incoming
matches your desired outgoing.

Monthly

Total Income   _____

Outgoing

Total of Absolutes   _____

Total of Absolutes Estimated   _____

Total of Yearly Absolutes   _____

Total of Personal and Family   _____

Total of Yearly Miscellaneous   _____

Total Outgoing   _____

Income – Total Outgoing =   _____

     $\div$ 4.333 = Weekly Savings   _____

If "Weekly Savings" is less than zero, then go back and cut back
in "Yearly Miscellaneous." If it is still less than zero, then go
back and cut back in "Personal and Family." If it is still less than
zero, cut anywhere else you can. If it is still less than zero, you
need another job or source of income.

USING SELF-CONTROL
TO MAKE MILLIONS

If you drink 3 Cokes a day = $4
7 days a week = $28
52 weeks a year = $1456

Year		Invested	Year		Invested
1	$1,456 =	$1,601.60	29 + $1,456 =		$232,303.40
2 + $1,456 =		$3,363.36	30 + $1,456 =		$257,135.34
3 + $1,456 =		$4,819.30	31 + $1,456 =		$284,450.47
4 + $1,456 =		$6,902.90	32 + $1,456 =		$314,497.11
5 + $1,456 =		$9,194.79	33 + $1,456 =		$347,548.42
6 + $1,456 =		$11,716.87	34 + $1,456 =		$383,904.86
7 + $1,456 =		$14,489.04	35 + $1,456 =		$423,896.94
8 + $1,456 =		$17,539.56	36 + $1,456 =		$467,888.23
9 + $1,456 =		$20,895.10	37 + $1,456 =		$516,278.65
10 + $1,456 =		$24,586.22	38 + $1,456 =		$569,508.11
11 + $1,456 =		$28,646.44	39 + $1,456 =		$628,060.52
12 + $1,456 =		$33,112.68	40 + $1,456 =		$692,060.52
13 + $1,456 =		$38,025.55	41 + $1,456 =		$763,316.58
14 + $1,456 =		$43,429.71	42 + $1,456 =		$841,249.83
15 + $1,456 =		$49,374.28	43 + $1,456 =		$926,976.41
16 + $1,456 =		$55,913.30	44 + $1,456 =		$1,021,275.60
17 + $1,456 =		$63,106.23	45 + $1,456 =		$1,125,004.70
18 + $1,456 =		$71,018.46	46 + $1,456 =		$1,239,106.70
19 + $1,456 =		$79,721.90	47 + $1,456 =		$1,364,618.90
20 + $1,456 =		$89,295.69	48 + $1,456 =		$1,502,682.30
21 + $1,456 =		$99,826.86	49 + $1,456 =		$1,654,552.10
22 + $1,456 =		$111,411.13	50 + $1,456 =		$1,821,608.90
23 + $1,456 =		$124,153.84	51 + $1,456 =		$2,005,371.30
24 + $1,456 =		$138,170.82	52 + $1,456 =		$2,207,510.00
25 + $1,456 =		$153,589.50	53 + $1,456 =		$2,429,862.60
26 + $1,456 =		$170,550.05	54 + $1,456 =		$2,674,450.40
27 + $1,456 =		$189,206.65	55 + $1,456 =		$2,943,497.00
28 + $1,456 =		$209,728.91			

USING SELF-CONTROL (CONT.)

For every $4 per day habit:

10 years = $25,000 in the bank
20 years = $90,000 in the bank
30 years = $260,000 in the bank
40 years = $700,000 in the bank
50 years = $1,900,000 in the bank
55 years = $3,000,000 in the bank

So if you smoke a pack a day, drink 3 sodas and eat fast food out 4 times a week (substitute a Starbucks a day for any of the three), it will cost you:

10 years = $75,000
20 years = $270,000
30 years = $780,000
40 years = $2,100,000
50 years = $5,700,000
55 years = $9,000,000

USING SELF-CONTROL (CONT.)

How many $4 a day addictions do you have?

_____   _____   _____

_____   _____   _____

_____   _____   _____

10 years:_____ x $25,000 = _____
        Number of addictions you have

20 years:_____ x $25,000 = _____
        Number of addictions you have

30 years:_____ x $25,000 = _____
        Number of addictions you have

40 years:_____ x $25,000 = _____
        Number of addictions you have

50 years:_____ x $25,000 = _____
        Number of addictions you have

55 years:_____ x $25,000 = _____
        Number of addictions you have

Money you will have if you give up and invest:

$_____

Invest:

If you invest 10% of your income, look what happens, even if you never get a raise. Example: You make $10 per hour; $400 a week. Invest $40 dollars a week in a simple investment.

$40 a week = 1.5 bad habits
In 55 years = $4,500
Now add that to giving up 3 bad habits:
55 years = $13,500,000

INTEGRITY/CREDIT

Let your yes be yes . . . (James 5:12)

Importance of Great Credit:

700 Score or Higher

Car Loan: $20,000

CREDIT	Great	Good	Average	Bad	Horrible
Interest:	3%	5%	7%	10%	27%
Payments Paid:	$360	$378	$396	$425	$610
Overall Interest:	$1,550	$2,646	$3,761	$5,500	$16,650

Great — Average = $1 a day or $1/4$ addiction = $750,000 lifetime.

Great — Bad = $2 a day or $1/2$ addiction = $1,500,000 lifetime.

Home Loan: $250,000

CREDIT	Great	Good	Average	Bad	Horrible
Interest:	3.8%	5%	6.5%	8.5%	None
Payments Paid:	$1,165	$1,342	$1,580	$1,922	Can't buy
Overall Interest:	$170,000	$233,120	$318,800	$442,000	

> Projected loss including tax deduction and 7% increased value of home:
> loss per month equals $2,115; $1,520,800 over 30 years.
> This equals 17 addictions or $53,000,000 in lifetime loss.

Great — Good = $6 a day or 1.25 bad habits = $3,750,000 lifetime.

Great — Average = $14 a day or 3.5 bad habits = $10,500,000 lifetime.

Great — Bad = $25 a day or 6 addictions = $18,000,000 lifetime.

Why buy a house?

A $250,000 house in five years is worth $350,638.

Profit	$100,637.93
Tax Savings	$26,393.40
Total	$127,031.33 a day or 18 addictions = $54,000,000 lifetime.

RAISE CREDIT SCORE

It is important that you know your credit score and manage it.

Http://loan.yahoo.com

To start credit:

1. _____

Then _____

2. _____

3. _____

What lowers score:

1. _____

To fix _____

_____

And _____

2. _____

3. _____

4. _____

5. _____

You need _____

Limit = _____

SAVE MILLIONS ON BUYING CARS

Why you never buy new!

Car drops $5,000 in value the moment you drive off lot.

Why you never buy off car lot(s)!

Purchased:	Private Sales	Car Lot
Vehicle:	2003 Tundra	2003 Tundra
Price:	$20,000	$20,000
Tax:	0	$1,530
Misc. Fees:	0	$250
Total:	$20,000	$21,780

Difference: $1,780

	Sell Your Car	Trade In
Vehicle:	99 Civic	99 Civic
Price:	$10,000	$6,000
$ Save on Tax:	0	$459

Difference: $5,321

Total Difference: $5,321

The average American gets a new car every two years. That is a loss of $7 a day, or two bad habits. Almost $5,250,000 lost in a lifetime.

Your car can be the worst investment or a great investment.

Vehicles depreciate at about 25% the first year, then 15% each year up to the fourth year.

Consider a $25,000 vehicle:

Year:	1	2	3	4
Value:	$18,750	$15,937	$13,546	$11,515
Loss:	$6,250	$9,063	$11,454	$13,485

If you own the vehicle for 2 years, it will cost you $12.41 a day or 3 bad habits, equaling $9,000,000 in a lifetime.

Why Not:
*Drive the car you want
*Make $1,000 a car
*Have a different car every 3-6 months

Keys:
1. Do not buy a car older than 4 years.
2. Do not buy a car with more than 60,000 miles.
3. Try to buy a vehicle that still has a factory warranty.
4. Never buy from a dealer.
5. Never buy a car with a salvage title.
6. Avoid vehicles with accidents on a CARFAX report unless you are getting it for an amazing deal.
7. Pray for God's favor, blessings and guidance.

Use AutoTrader.com to find a vehicle.

Use www.kbb.com to find out what the vehicle's value is.

Key:

For me to even consider a vehicle, it must be priced $1,000 or more below private-party value (usually $1,500). I then offer $1,000 below that and, worst case scenerio, get the vehicle at $1,500 below book.

Make sure you spend $30 to get a CARFAX report!

Things to ask and look for while looking at a vehicle:
1. Check tires (new tires will cost you $400-$800).
2. Does it leak fluid?
3. Any weird noises?
4. Make sure you drive on freeway.
5. When were the brakes serviced last?
6. Ever been in any accidents?
7. Does it have a salvage title?
   (Ask questions 6 and 7 over the phone so you don't waste your time.)
8. Check all power gadgets. Make sure they work.
9. If you are mechanically challenged, spend $100 and have a mechanic check the vehicle out for you.

The same day you buy the vehicle, put it into the Auto Trader. Price vehicle at $250 below book and drive it until it sells.

Profit usually is $500-$1,500 a vehicle.
I average $1,000 every three months.

$4,000 a year or $11 a day or 2.75 bad habits.

$8,219,178 lifetime.
$9,000,000 I don't lose like the rest of America.
$17,219,178 lifetime.

THE BEAUTY OF THE RETIREMENT PLAN

When you contribute to a 401(k) or 403(b) the money deposited into your retirement account is taken from your PRE-TAXED earnings.

	Retirement plan 401(k) Pre tax	Regular way to do it
Gross Income	$15 an hour = $600	$15 an hour = $600
Amount to go in retirement account	8% of $600 = $48	0
Typical employer's match	25% of what you put in $12	0
Amount of paycheck after taxes and retirement deduction	$386.40	$420
Difference	$33.60 less per week	$33.60 more per week
Amount in retirement	$60 per week	$0 per week
Difference	$60-$33.60 = $26.40 more per week or $1,372.80 a year plus the 10% interest gained makes it $1,510.08 a year.	$60-$33.60 = $26.40 less per week
Which equals how many bad habits?	Almost one full bad habit	
Money over a lifetime	$2,800,000	

Notice that even without the employer's match, it is still $14.40 a month more money—Over $800 a year more money. This is one half a bad habit or $1,500,000 in a lifetime.

Fact: When an employer matches a percentage of your retirement investment, it is like getting an instant raise. If it is a 50% match, then for every $100 you put in, they put in $50. That can work out to quite a raise over time.

Mon	Where did the time go? What you did:

See then that you walk circumspectly, not as fools
but as wise, redeeming the time. (Ephesians 5:15-16)

6-7 am _____

7-8 am _____

8-9 am _____

9-10 am _____

10-11 am _____

11-12 pm _____

12-1 pm _____

1-2 pm _____

2-3 pm _____

3-4 pm _____

4-5 pm _____

5-6 pm _____

6-7 pm _____

7-8 pm _____

8-9 pm _____

9-10 pm _____

10-11 pm _____

11-12 am _____

12-1 am _____

1-2 am _____

2-3 am _____

3-4 am _____

4-5 am _____

5-6 am _____

| Tue | Where did the time go? What you did: |

*See then that you walk circumspectly, not as fools
but as wise, redeeming the time. (Ephesians 5:15-16)*

6-7 am _____

7-8 am _____

8-9 am _____

9-10 am _____

10-11 am _____

11-12 pm _____

12-1 pm _____

1-2 pm _____

2-3 pm _____

3-4 pm _____

4-5 pm _____

5-6 pm _____

6-7 pm _____

7-8 pm _____

8-9 pm _____

9-10 pm _____

10-11 pm _____

11-12 am _____

12-1 am _____

1-2 am _____

2-3 am _____

3-4 am _____

4-5 am _____

5-6 am _____

Wed	Where did the time go? What you did:

See then that you walk circumspectly, not as fools
but as wise, redeeming the time. (Ephesians 5:15-16)

6-7am _____

7-8am _____

8-9am _____

9-10am _____

10-11am _____

11-12pm _____

12-1pm _____

1-2pm _____

2-3pm _____

3-4pm _____

4-5pm _____

5-6pm _____

6-7pm _____

7-8pm _____

8-9pm _____

9-10pm _____

10-11pm _____

11-12am _____

12-1am _____

1-2am _____

2-3am _____

3-4am _____

4-5am _____

5-6am _____

Thu | Where did the time go? What you did:

See then that you walk circumspectly, not as fools
but as wise, redeeming the time. (Ephesians 5:15-16)

6-7 am _____

7-8 am _____

8-9 am _____

9-10 am _____

10-11 am _____

11-12 pm _____

12-1 pm _____

1-2 pm _____

2-3 pm _____

3-4 pm _____

4-5 pm _____

5-6 pm _____

6-7 pm _____

7-8 pm _____

8-9 pm _____

9-10 pm _____

10-11 pm _____

11-12 am _____

12-1 am _____

1-2 am _____

2-3 am _____

3-4 am _____

4-5 am _____

5-6 am _____

Fri	Where did the time go? What you did:

See then that you walk circumspectly, not as fools
but as wise, redeeming the time. (Ephesians 5:15-16)

6-7 am _____

7-8 am _____

8-9 am _____

9-10 am _____

10-11 am _____

11-12 pm _____

12-1 pm _____

1-2 pm _____

2-3 pm _____

3-4 pm _____

4-5 pm _____

5-6 pm _____

6-7 pm _____

7-8 pm _____

8-9 pm _____

9-10 pm _____

10-11 pm _____

11-12 am _____

12-1 am _____

1-2 am _____

2-3 am _____

3-4 am _____

4-5 am _____

5-6 am _____

Sat	Where did the time go? What you did:

See then that you walk circumspectly, not as fools
but as wise, redeeming the time. (Ephesians 5:15-16)

6-7 am _____

7-8 am _____

8-9 am _____

9-10 am _____

10-11 am _____

11-12 pm _____

12-1 pm _____

1-2 pm _____

2-3 pm _____

3-4 pm _____

4-5 pm _____

5-6 pm _____

6-7 pm _____

7-8 pm _____

8-9 pm _____

9-10 pm _____

10-11 pm _____

11-12 am _____

12-1 am _____

1-2 am _____

2-3 am _____

3-4 am _____

4-5 am _____

5-6 am _____

Sun	Where did the time go? What you did:

*See then that you walk circumspectly, not as fools
but as wise, redeeming the time. (Ephesians 5:15-16)*

6-7 am _____

7-8 am _____

8-9 am _____

9-10 am _____

10-11 am _____

11-12 pm _____

12-1 pm _____

1-2 pm _____

2-3 pm _____

3-4 pm _____

4-5 pm _____

5-6 pm _____

6-7 pm _____

7-8 pm _____

8-9 pm _____

9-10 pm _____

10-11 pm _____

11-12 am _____

12-1 am _____

1-2 am _____

2-3 am _____

3-4 am _____

4-5 am _____

5-6 am _____

Key:

Go back and mark the following:

M — Must-Do Time (work, eat, shower, drive, etc.)

R — Relax Time

S — Sleep Time

V — Vision and Personal Growth

W — Wasted Time

E — Errands

F — Friends and Relationship Time

Where Time Went:		Total Time		Per Day % by 7
M — Must-Do Time	=		=	
R — Relax Time	=		=	
S — Sleep Time	=		=	
V — Vision and Personal Growth	=		=	
W — Wasted Time	=		=	
E — Errands	=		=	
F — Friends and Relationship	=		=	

Based on this report, is your time going appropriately towards your vision and dream? (When "Relax Time" is greater than "Vision Time," you will never reach your vision.)

What changes must you make?

Now go back and place the symbols below next to time you can change.

Key 2:

? — Time that could be vision
* — Time that could be *combined* with vision

Based on this information, write out next week's schedule.

> *Then the LORD answered me and said:*
>   *"Write the vision*
>   *And make it plain on tablets,*
>   *That he may run who reads it."*
>   (Habakkuk 2:2)

| Mon | Where did the time go? What you did: |

*See then that you walk circumspectly, not as fools
but as wise, redeeming the time. (Ephesians 5:15-16)*

6-7 am _____

7-8 am _____

8-9 am _____

9-10 am _____

10-11 am _____

11-12 pm _____

12-1 pm _____

1-2 pm _____

2-3 pm _____

3-4 pm _____

4-5 pm _____

5-6 pm _____

6-7 pm _____

7-8 pm _____

8-9 pm _____

9-10 pm _____

10-11 pm _____

11-12 am _____

12-1 am _____

1-2 am _____

2-3 am _____

3-4 am _____

4-5 am _____

5-6 am _____

Tue | Where did the time go? What you did:

See then that you walk circumspectly, not as fools
but as wise, redeeming the time. (Ephesians 5:15-16)

6-7 am _____

7-8 am _____

8-9 am _____

9-10 am _____

10-11 am _____

11-12 pm _____

12-1 pm _____

1-2 pm _____

2-3 pm _____

3-4 pm _____

4-5 pm _____

5-6 pm _____

6-7 pm _____

7-8 pm _____

8-9 pm _____

9-10 pm _____

10-11 pm _____

11-12 am _____

12-1 am _____

1-2 am _____

2-3 am _____

3-4 am _____

4-5 am _____

5-6 am _____

Wed | Where did the time go? What you did:

See then that you walk circumspectly, not as fools
but as wise, redeeming the time. (Ephesians 5:15-16)

6-7 am _____

7-8 am _____

8-9 am _____

9-10 am _____

10-11 am _____

11-12 pm _____

12-1 pm _____

1-2 pm _____

2-3 pm _____

3-4 pm _____

4-5 pm _____

5-6 pm _____

6-7 pm _____

7-8 pm _____

8-9 pm _____

9-10 pm _____

10-11 pm _____

11-12 am _____

12-1 am _____

1-2 am _____

2-3 am _____

3-4 am _____

4-5 am _____

5-6 am _____

Thu | Where did the time go? What you did:

See then that you walk circumspectly, not as fools
but as wise, redeeming the time. (Ephesians 5:15-16)

6-7 am _____

7-8 am _____

8-9 am _____

9-10 am _____

10-11 am _____

11-12 pm _____

12-1 pm _____

1-2 pm _____

2-3 pm _____

3-4 pm _____

4-5 pm _____

5-6 pm _____

6-7 pm _____

7-8 pm _____

8-9 pm _____

9-10 pm _____

10-11 pm _____

11-12 am _____

12-1 am _____

1-2 am _____

2-3 am _____

3-4 am _____

4-5 am _____

5-6 am _____

Fri Where did the time go? What you did:

See then that you walk circumspectly, not as fools
but as wise, redeeming the time. (Ephesians 5:15-16)

6-7 am _____

7-8 am _____

8-9 am _____

9-10 am _____

10-11 am _____

11-12 pm _____

12-1 pm _____

1-2 pm _____

2-3 pm _____

3-4 pm _____

4-5 pm _____

5-6 pm _____

6-7 pm _____

7-8 pm _____

8-9 pm _____

9-10 pm _____

10-11 pm _____

11-12 am _____

12-1 am _____

1-2 am _____

2-3 am _____

3-4 am _____

4-5 am _____

5-6 am _____

Sat | Where did the time go? What you did:

See then that you walk circumspectly, not as fools
but as wise, redeeming the time. (Ephesians 5:15-16)

6-7 am _____

7-8 am _____

8-9 am _____

9-10 am _____

10-11 am _____

11-12 pm _____

12-1 pm _____

1-2 pm _____

2-3 pm _____

3-4 pm _____

4-5 pm _____

5-6 pm _____

6-7 pm _____

7-8 pm _____

8-9 pm _____

9-10 pm _____

10-11 pm _____

11-12 am _____

12-1 am _____

1-2 am _____

2-3 am _____

3-4 am _____

4-5 am _____

5-6 am _____

Sun	Where did the time go? What you did:

See then that you walk circumspectly, not as fools but as wise, redeeming the time. (Ephesians 5:15-16)

6-7 am _____

7-8 am _____

8-9 am _____

9-10 am _____

10-11 am _____

11-12 pm _____

12-1 pm _____

1-2 pm _____

2-3 pm _____

3-4 pm _____

4-5 pm _____

5-6 pm _____

6-7 pm _____

7-8 pm _____

8-9 pm _____

9-10 pm _____

10-11 pm _____

11-12 am _____

12-1 am _____

1-2 am _____

2-3 am _____

3-4 am _____

4-5 am _____

5-6 am _____

NOW GO DO IT!

There are millions of ways to make your billions. I made my money in real estate. This is not the only way, but for me it was a good way. I spent hundreds of hours researching, reading, listening, and then I stepped out into it. For you, it might be another way, but it is important that you get understanding on the way. Get all the books and tapes and information you can get. Get understanding and wisdom concerning your endeavor. Now step out. Start that corporation, buy those stocks, those bonds, invent that thing. Whatever God has put into your heart, step out and cast that net and grab that harvest. Now you are blessed. Make sure you are always a blessing.

ABOUT THE AUTHOR
Scot Anderson

 After interviewing numerous multi-millionaires, reading more than twenty books on becoming a millionaire and listening to nearly 400 hours of CDs on obtaining wealth, Scot came to a conclusion: Billionaires think differently than the rest of us. This book is his journey, his notes, and the thinking he changed. Take this journey with him; change the thinking in you. Begin to think like a Billionaire, and your life will have no choice but to produce it.